The Evacuee

Who Became a St. Ivian

To Kathie & Larry

For your unfailing devotion
& belief that I could
do it

Raymond Cole

Feb 07

The Evacuee

Who Became a St. Ivian

The personal story of a boy's remembrances
and experiences after being evacuated from
London to St. Ives as an evacuee
in September 1939

Raymond L. Pole

iUniverse, Inc.
New York Lincoln Shanghai

The Evacuee Who Became a St. Ivian

iUniverse books may be ordered through booksellers or by contacting:

iUniverse
2021 Pine Lake Road, Suite 100
Lincoln, NE 68512
www.iuniverse.com
1-800-Authors (1-800-288-4677)

ISBN-13: 978-0-595-40876-4 (pbk)
ISBN-13: 978-0-595-85239-0 (ebk)
ISBN-10: 0-595-40876-1 (pbk)
ISBN-10: 0-595-85239-4 (ebk)

Printed in the United States of America

To My Dear Mother

Sarah Anne Pole

and all mothers

who gave up their children to save them

and to

Freddie Favell

A Townsman of St. Ives

Acknowledgement is conveyed to Kevin Robinson for the use of his painting of St. Ives Bridge in 1939 on the cover of this book.

Contents

Introduction & Acknowledgements

Writing a story, especially about oneself, is certainly a new experience for me and quite different from the technical reports and surveys I have written in the course of my career. I had to work much harder to create a flow of ideas, feelings, and reactions, rather than just relating a series of incidents and recollections from a bygone age. To bring about a balance between facts and sentiments, I needed to wrestle with my left and right brain. To help me in this process, my love and appreciation goes to my wife Beth and to Kathie Yaggi, who helped me in this process of preserving the authenticity of my recollections and still capture the right sensitivity for today's readers. Margaret Allen in Wales also did a great job of changing my American spelling back to English style, since the reminiscences and reflections all originated when I was an English boy.

When I found my original manuscript done in 1992, I discovered that it had been saved on a floppy diskette in a now obsolete program. My thanks and appreciation goes to Larry Yaggi who patiently scanned each page into a workable document and onto a CD that I could edit.

I owe a great deal of thanks to my friend Brad Fregger who encouraged me in the early stages as a non-writer to stick with it and to recall not only facts but to release all the emotions and feelings I was still harbouring. To Kathie Yaggi, Diana Aldrich and Beth who patiently checked and rechecked every page and every word many times to get it right. To David Ogilvie, my brother-in-law, who added his artistic touch by recreating the map of St. Ives as I knew it, together with a sketch of the statue of St. Ives most famous townsman of the past.

Foreword

Raymond Pole's narrative describes an important time in the local history of St. Ives. This was typical of the dramatic changes that occurred at the beginning of the war in small towns throughout England.

Looking back through the past 60 years of unbroken peace in Western Europe, it seems amazing that within living memory of millions of people, in London and many British cities, who were threatened with ruthless destruction at the hands of another European country. Dreadful as the eventual bombing of those cities was, there existed amongst the government and local authorities, the initial fear and possibility of a poison gas attack which precipitated the need for mass evacuation even before war was declared. This concern was also evident from the circulation of gas masks in 1938.

Families were broken up as city children were suddenly taken away from their parents and sent to the safety of the countryside. Small towns were selected that could be served by railways as the most economical way to execute such a formidable project.

The ongoing trauma of the early war years affected everyone from the draft into war-work or the armed forces, to the reduction of food supplies, and only those who lived through this period with the constant fear of being invaded, remembered, but seldom ever talk about it now.

Raymond Pole was one of those children and this is his story. His strength of character meant that he was able to gain something positive from this experience, and his equally good memory has enabled him to record it for us and for the enlightenment of his peers and their children.

A townsman of St. Ives, Cambridgeshire, England

Preface

With the threat of war with Germany in 1938, and the fear of poison gas being used, the government organized a plan to evacuate all the schools and children living in London (and later other cities that were deemed to be potential targets) to places away from the large industrial towns to small rural areas that could be reached easily by train.

It has struck me as I have grown up that becoming "an evacuee" and obeying the will of the government, was really a unique situation that does not happen very often in one's lifetime and that it was an historical fact. So it was not difficult to respond to the question, "What was a significant time in your life and why?" With over sixty years on which to reflect on this question, I came to the conclusion that the evacuation experience, from 1939 to 1944, was a very significant time for me. It was also a traumatic change for many who were around the same age, which had both positive and negative effects at a very formative time of a young person's life. I did not realize until years later that this forced adventure offered me an escape from strict parental control and allowed me a freedom that I am not sure I was mature enough to handle. I was coming to an age where I was beginning to question and challenge, but there was little I could do about it. It was in this setting that the sudden opportunity for freedom to express myself was thrust upon me. Following my own desires was not always a good thing and at times I became worse off. This sudden "coming of age" although only eleven, and being unplanned, had a profound effect on me at an impressionable time in my life.

Another reason to "tell my story" was to create a record of some of the precious moments in time, of people, places and incidents, that unless captured in print, would perhaps disappear forever. It is easy to see that future generations would never know what happened to change the course of daily living for thousands of people and particularly to me and my friends, as we were whisked away to this English country town of St. Ives in the county of Huntingdonshire.

I have a tremendous sense of gratitude for the people of St. Ives and many other local people of towns and villages all over the country who went through a similar experience at the beginning of World War II. It was a "people-to-people" experience that may never be repeated. It was widely understood that country people in those days were somewhat apprehensive about big city kids and perhaps we were viewed as wild kids from the asphalt jungles.

To find foster parents to house and take care of strange children, was a formidable undertaking. Who could possibly understand and readily agree to respond to the national bulletins being issued to prepare for such an emergency. War had not yet been declared but the government was quite sure that our cities would be bombed and poison gas used. They made it very clear that action must be taken to evacuate one and a half million children, teachers and adult-aids within four days to villages and small towns that could be easily accessed by rail. It is also important to me that my story be told for the people of St. Ives as well as for other evacuees who had gone through similar traumas.

Living in America for over forty-five years, I have become aware that although the United States war started with the bombing of Pearl Harbor on December 7, 1941, few Americans really knew about the significance of September 3, 1939, in Britain, let alone September 1, 1939. This personal story may be enlightening to many in America as they become aware how dramatic this period was in our English history. Americans were generally in awe to learn about the separation of children from their parents and the difficulty for young children to adapt to strange environments as they changed from being young children into young teenagers.

Finally, I want to share some personal feelings and anecdotes with my children and grandchildren in written form, thinking that perhaps reading about such things is really the preferred way rather than to keep on verbalizing about one's young life.

For fifty years, many of these memories lay dormant as my wife and I went about the daily task of raising our children in California—until I saw the film "Hope and Glory," which was directed by John Boorman who recollected his own wartime childhood experiences through the character of Billy Rohan and acted out by Sebastian Rice Edwards. I began thinking and even saying out loud, "Wow, he was speaking just like me," as I watched and experienced the happenings being portrayed by a boy whose mother would not let him be evacuated. Nevertheless, he had experienced the traumas of being bombed and the daily exploits of that era together with a dialogue that was typically from London. Many of my feelings were also reinforced by the character Kevin Arnold, as played by the young actor, Fred Savage in the 1989-90 TV series, "The Wonder Years." Such emotions and dialogue being acted out then helped me to get in touch with how a 12-year-old thinks and behaves. The inner-voice and thoughts, being played out by the actor made the story very unique and different than what was actually being conveyed in the moment. It was through these two characters that I was encouraged to reconstruct in vivid detail, some of the many incidents that I could remember when I was at that same age.

It was with much trepidation that I dared to seek out anyone in 1989 outside my peer group who could substantiate the occurrences of half a century ago, realizing that most of the adults I knew then may have passed away. On this visit back to St. Ives marking the fiftieth anniversary of the evacuation and the declaration of the war, we did locate Freddie Favell, whom I could still recognize as possibly the only person who could, as the billeting officer at that time, substantiate, not only the sequence of events on evacuation day in 1939, but give me some insight of the unprecedented drama he experienced in trying to find enough homes for this sudden influx of population. I am very pleased to dedicate this book to Mr. Favell and his contemporaries.

Many history books are available to record the facts surrounding the life and times of Oliver Cromwell but, for me, no one tells the story as well as Dr. L. Du Garde Peach, whose book *Oliver Cromwell*, published by Ladybird Books Ltd., provides much on his relationship with St. Ives and the mark he left there some three hundred years ago. So, too, did the era of the evacuees coming to St. Ives, leave an indelible mark on the town and its citizens some sixty years ago. As so typical in England, it takes some traumatic events to affect the status-quo of small towns such as St. Ives, with these particular events, and I believe that I have attempted to relate some of these to you.

May this simple autobiography be added to the annals of the history of St. Ives. I extend my deepest thanks, appreciation and dedication to all the people I have mentioned that made a difference to my life.

Raymond L. Pole
September, 2006
Sunnyvale, California U.S.A.

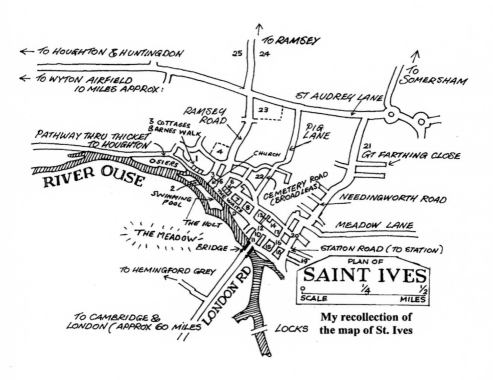

My recollection of
the map of St. Ives

Location of places mentioned in this narrative and marked on our map:

1. Barnes Walk and the Three Cottages
2. Swimming Pool: (with river water flowing through island)
3. All Saints Parish Church and adjacent Vicarage
4. The Anderson's Family Farm
5. Anglers Rest, (Bed & Breakfast)
6. Harry Anderson's Butcher Shop
7. The Bell Bar
8. The Methodist Church on the Waits
9. Norris Museum
10. Barton's, Chemist Shop
11. George Anderson's Butcher Shop
12. Crown Cross, the center crossroads from Bridge Street, Broadway & Market Hill, (with an Alley connecting into East St.)
13. Slaughter House off East Street
14. Corn Exchange
15. Free Church, and our Boys School in the Church Halls
16. Oliver Cromwell Statue and the Golden Lion Hotel
17. Stiles Baker Shop
18. Clements Newspaper Shop
19. W.H. Smith & Son Paper Shop at the Station
20. Area of Livestock Market
21. Mr. Woodhorn's House
22. Cemetery and #7 Cemetery Road
23. Jerry Anderson's Chicken Farm
24. Grandpa Anderson's House
25. The Sims' House

Chapter One

Evacuation Day
September 1, 1939

We, in London, had been building up this expectancy for over a month, as each day during August of 1939, the children were told to be prepared to move out "On One Day's Notice." My mother, who was not use to preparing sandwiches for three children every school day for a month, must have been under a lot of stress to maintain this simple task plus the decision of what to put into them, notwithstanding the implications that this need implied. It must have been trying for all parents and school teachers to maintain a sense of well-being as well as a state of readiness, at a time when politicians and newspapers were heavy with more serious matters pertaining to the conflicts that were occurring throughout Europe.

Most of the kids were full of apprehension concerning the future and yet excited for the adventure it could bring. Some of us were unhappy that for the second year running our holidays had been cut short, and we had to attend summer school. Besides, this whole nasty business was messing up the cricket season. I remember very well, the same thing happened in August 1938, only then my mother was told she had to provide sleeping bags for us all. Since we could not afford to purchase such luxuries, this entailed sewing sheets and blankets into a bedroll which was pretty heavy to balance on top of one's rucksack. Thank goodness we were not required to provide our own bedding in 1939.

The older people must have been very fearful because many had gone through this type of drama during the "Great War" and really knew the horrors of such conflicts. The military reserves were also standing by to move out on short notice, so the atmosphere in London during the month of August was tense, to say the least.

September 1, 1939, was certainly the action day for all Londoners. It was very remarkable and a credit to the authorities that thousands of school children were all marshalled, two-by-two outside every school throughout London, and led off by the proverbial Pied-Piper to their nearest train station. There were dozens of weeping mothers at the train stations that Friday morning, even though they were told by the school teachers not to come, but to say their "good-byes" at the school gates. You can imagine the pandemonium to get several hundred children, between 5 and 15 years old, each with their rucksack, gas mask and a paper bag containing their sandwiches, on to the trains.

While the destinations were "top-secret," we knew when we saw those strange sounding names on the station platforms, as the train sped through, that we must be "way out" in the country. Huntingdon was only 60 miles north of London, but it was still a long way for us. Some children were evacuated to Cornwall in Devon and North Wales, away from the cities and industrial centres of Great Britain.

At the Huntingdon Station, we were grouped together by schools and allocated to different buses bound for the surrounding towns and villages. Our school, Highbury Vale Elementary, joined by the Blackstock Road Elementary School (located less than a mile from us in London), were headed for the small country town called St. Ives. We were given some emergency rations such as tins of corned beef, condensed milk and jam, a bar of Cadbury's chocolate and a few other essential commodities that everyone was trailing around in very large carrier bags. It must have been late afternoon by the time we reached our destination, and we were getting hungry as most children had eaten their sandwiches on the train earlier that day.

The billeting officer in St. Ives was Mr. Freddie Favell who stood on an auctioneer's platform in the town's Corn Exchange, and proceeded to call out names to pair-up the evacuees with their host families. Slowly the meeting hall began to empty and in the corner were three anxious children who were not yet called. My mother told me we must not be split up, so I made this point clear when attempts were made to separate us.

Apparently, no one wanted three children of our age span, for my sister was eight and my brother was only six years old.

In the end, a venerable old man in his eighties, an alderman by the name of Mr. Woodhorn, opened his home as a temporary haven, unbeknown to his young housekeeper who was not so pleased at the prospect of suddenly becoming a "mother." After a good supper we were ready to climb into those palatial beds provided by our kindly host. We really became unpopular when the next morning my little brother Gerard dropped the rather full chamber pot in his attempt to empty it in the bathroom. Then a few days later, my sister Huguette developed an ear infection. The frustrated housekeeper just could not cope with this dramatic change to her daily routine, so the billeting officer had to find us another home.

On our second day in these new surroundings, I was up early eager to explore the neighborhood. My friend Donald must have had the same idea because we met on the country road near the farm at the top of Needingworth Road where he had been billeted. After comparing notes on our respective homes and the people who lived there, we noticed many planes flying around and could see in the distance that they were landing and taking off again. It did not take us long to decide to find out from where all this activity was originating, and off we went up the Houghton Road to discover the Wyton Aerodrome. We found an open gate and wandered on to the tarmac to see the planes up close. Wow! We couldn't wait to tell the other kids how we had actually talked to the pilots, and for sure our stories became more exaggerated the more we repeated our escapade.

I remember hitching a ride home (which was another new experience) and discovering how anxious our new foster parents had been, believing that perhaps we were trying to walk back to London since we had disappeared for over two hours.

On Sunday morning, the 3rd of September 1939, I got dressed in my Sunday best and went with Mr. Woodhorn to the parish church. As we came out of the service, we stopped by a house near the river and from the open window at 11:15 a.m. we heard the Prime Minister, Mr. Neville Chamberlain's speech and his "Declaration of War" with Germany. It had finally happened and all this talk and apprehension was now a reality. While I was old enough to accept the seriousness of the state affairs, it never occurred to me that this was to be such a turning point in world history and a moment in time around which millions of people would record and reflect their reactions. It was three memorable days in the life of an eleven-year-old that will never be forgotten.

We were eventually relocated from the Woodhorn residence and my sister was placed with another older girl and Gerard and I went to live with the Sims family who lived in a council house on the top of Ramsay Road. Huguette was very unhappy there so Mrs. Sims said she could come and live with us. However, that meant we all had to sleep in the same room.

Mr. Sims worked in outdoor construction, and their only daughter was working at the local mill. While they did accept us at first, I believe that they soon realised that they had taken on a very big responsibility and perhaps the persuasiveness of the billeting officer to keep us there, was beginning to wear thin.

Whenever my mother came on a Sunday to visit us, she would bring a "joint" (i.e. *a joint of meat suitable for roasting for the whole family*). I think this pleased Mrs. Sims to receive such a meaningful contribution towards a good Sunday dinner.

After six to eight months away from home, my Mother and Dad decided to take my sister and brother back to London. With the actual war being confined to the European mainland, life in England at that time, did not seem to present too many hardships. The anxieties that predicated the massive evacuation were not so acute in the early months of 1940. In their place, however, many problems were arising with the children living in foster homes. The novelty was wearing thin, and feelings were surfacing between the foster parents and the real parents, when the fear of life and limb was not so apparent.

While the perception that the foster parents may have had about the London parents not having the daily worries and tribulations associated with bringing up children, thus giving them the freedom to pursue voluntary duties and war-work, it also became evident, in many instances, that resentments were building up with the foster parents over the financial burden of housing someone else's children together with the added time and responsibility of caring for children belonging to strangers. (There was a government token allowance given for every child).

There must have been real concern by some parents who missed their children very much, and not sensing a real danger in the moment, yielded to the temptation to bring their children back home.

Such was the case in my family, when my parents learned that my seven-year-old brother was found in a boat floating down the river on his own. When I look back on such incidents, they hardly sound real, and for certain it was a big responsibility to place on foster parents. Gerard was by nature an inquisitive boy who was very active, and he loved to explore. Inevitably he got into trouble. Most of the time these common escapades of unsupervised activities, were harmless encounters, which nevertheless, did bring about many moments of anguish to our foster parents and eventually to our parents.

My sister was a very shy and sweet little nine-year-old, who had been studying ballet and tap dancing and who was now forgetting her routines and losing the rhythm without the discipline of weekly classes. She missed her "Maman" most of all, and when Mother found her daughter with so many torn clothes, I believe that this was the deciding factor to take her and my brother back home to London.

Chapter Two

Shared Reminiscences for the Fiftieth Anniversary in 1989

*R*eturning to England from California in August 1989, I was amazed at the publicity in all the papers that was beginning to build up for this fifty-year anniversary date. Authors must have been hard at work for months, preparing special books on the events surrounding the outbreak of the war and three or four were even dedicated to the trauma of the evacuation of children. It never occurred to me that in reality, many thousands of young people must have had very similar experiences. In fact, it became uncanny that so many people had recorded similar events in such detail about what happened on that memorable day.

When my open invitation to a reunion appeared in the local Huntingdon county paper, I too received many responses. One reader phoned and inquired, "Was this the same Raymond Pole who sang as a choir boy in St. John's Church in Highbury, London?" (He was, but how was the editor to know that?) He invited the inquirer to also relate his own experiences on the evacuation, and so started an appeal for more stories. Soon this paper along with hundreds of other papers, both local and national, were recalling special events and memories of fifty years ago, not just on the evacuation day but on many scenarios surrounding the beginning of the war. The radio was playing nostalgic music from the forties and the BBC created and repeated many programs of these important events, even to excerpts of the news at that time.

Remember the news announcer who always said, "This is the News, and this is Alvar Liddell reading it?" which was preceded by the familiar six pips.

In my article, I invited anyone who could recall this same day and was available to meet with me in the Golden Lion Hotel in St. Ives. Six people who were original evacuees, turned up for this blind date, together with their spouses plus some of the local people who had received us "London kids" long ago.

We talked non-stop for three hours. It was intriguing that although we were all fifty years older and considerably changed in appearance, the recognition came through as we related little stories each of us could remember that we had in common. One person said, "Do you remember that poor boy who was always getting caned by the headmaster and what a 'pantomime' that was?" He was small for his age of 10 and when asked to put out his hand at arm's length, he would pull it back just before the cane would hit his palm. This would continue for several times, and all could see the teacher's blood pressure rising. Eventually, in sheer desperation the teacher made him lean over the desk and he would pound his "bum". The class did not know whether to laugh at the antics or cry in sympathy with his yells. Most of the other boys would take this type of corporal punishment "like a man and would return to their seats and sit on their hands in an attempt to kill the pain" … and so the reminiscences continued.

The presence of Ronnie Guest at the reunion, along with his brother George and their respective wives, was a surprise. Ronnie was so excited about the whole affair that he, too, wrote to the Hunts Herald and Post and this is what they printed:

"I certainly remember my very first day in St. Ives. It was Friday, September 1, 1939, and my brothers Teddy, George and I were staying in one of the cottages on St. George's Street. After lunch we all went exploring around the churchyard area and playing alongside the river. I had been there only ten minutes, when I fell in. Being a non-swimmer then, it certainly gave me a fright but fortunately, my brothers managed to pull me out. I felt a 'right Charlie' having to walk back to my new home dripping wet. I was expecting to get a real wallop from the people I was staying with, but they were so very kind and understanding."

Ronnie continued "Since we were really very over-crowded, I eventually went to live with the people who managed the Regal Cinema and spent many happy months with them. Eventually, my brothers and I returned to London just in time for the coming blitz (the continuous nightly bombing of London)."

Yes, I too, had many fond memories of the local Regal Cinema. They changed the main feature three times a week, with one performance a day plus a matinee on Saturday afternoon. Films like *Gunga Din and Destry Rides Again* come to mind, and who could forget *Hopalong Cassidy*. The very distinctive voice of the commentator who gave us the *Gaumont British News* became ingrained into our memories as we watched the world events three times a week. Ronnie had the envious job of being an usher and could see all the pictures for free. Later he was promoted to operate the projector and, of course, he became very popular with his school friends who were hoping that he would slip them inside the cinema without paying the sixpence or shilling entrance ticket. Ronnie's foster parents were kind and generous, so he did not abuse the free passes he was allowed for his brothers.

Talking about the local pictures, I can recall a very special friend whose name was Charlie; he was an older person whom I had met from the Parish Church. He enjoyed going to the pictures, and whenever he saw me queuing up to go in, he would pay for me and this made me feel very special.

Ronnie told us during our day of reunion that his first home in St. Ives was not so good. He and four other boys were billeted with a couple and their daughter who lived over one of the shops on Bridge Street. The boys were literally herded into a small bedroom so one can imagine the rumpus that caused.

Ronnie related that when his mother came up from London and saw the situation, "my Mum went potty" at the dirty conditions, particularly over the one towel shared by five boys. Ronnie's Mum grabbed him by the collar and took off in search of the headmaster's house to demand that alternative accommodation be found for her son.

The other recollection that Ronnie shared about those digs was that their host family always ate different food than was prepared for the boys. He recalls that their main menu was often faggots and pease pudding*. This meal was considered a treat back home in London, but to eat it almost every day for a month made them all very depressed. Taking in so many kids produced a nice income from the government's allowance which, I'm sure, some people took advantage of, while others gave more to their adopted children than ever could have been repaid, and loved doing it.

George Guest recalled the joy of his birthday of August 26, 1939, and one week later being uprooted from his familiar surroundings and

---

* Note: faggots, a seasoned panfry made with liver or scraps of pigs offal and sometimes pressed into round balls and wrapped with pigs caul fat. Pease pudding was a vegetable made with dried split peas.

family environment and taken to this far away place. He told the following story:

"Being the eldest of three brothers, I was told by my Mum to keep together and not to become separated. Having this responsibility was something new and, at times, I must have become quite bossy. We were billeted with a couple who appeared much older than our parents, and although they were very kind to us, three extra sons were really too much for them, so we had to move to new homes. Ronnie and I went to people up the Houghton Road while my other brother Ted got fixed up at the local Barber's home but later went to stay with a retired Postman not far from where we lived. I was relieved that we were still close so that I could keep an eye on things. Ted's family treated him well and, after some time, wrote to my parents with a proposal to adopt Ted. This, of course, was turned down, and then their attitude changed causing my parents to take Ted home. I was never really happy in my new home, and going to school and playing with my friends was a relief from the feeling of not being wanted. Eventually, we all went back to London and faced the blitz together (when the continuous bombing kept up for days), and although scary at times, we had the security of being a family."

Ronnie with his wife and family now live in Warboys and George and his family live in the village of March (both places near St. Ives) so the countryside must have had some lure for both these boys to return with their families, many years later.

Alex Rolfe came to the reunion and, although younger than myself, I did remember him and his older brother who was then very protective of Alex. His parents lived in Highbury Quadrant opposite our house in London. His Dad went into the armed services and his mother did war work. Gradually, the boys became estranged from their parents and were accepted more by their foster parents. At the end of the war, they found out that their parents had moved and had become divorced. Alex returned to St. Ives to the only family he had known and, henceforth, they adopted him. Now fifty years later, he is taking care of his adopted parents, which is rather touching.

Another evacuee was Mrs. J. Haswell, now living in St. Neots, who also came to St. Ives on Evacuation Day and stayed for three years before returning to London in 1942. She wrote to the Hunts Herald and Post: "I must have known Mr. Pole as we came from the same area in London and, being the same age, must have attended the same class at school, although I cannot recall his name. Fifty years is a long time, but I should very much like to attend the function at the Golden Lion. I am sure we have some memories to talk about. By some strange coincidence, I returned to live in St. Neots twenty-seven years ago when the firm my husband worked for, moved here from Park Royal. Although married with children and grandchildren I still have warm recollections of my stay in St. Ives. I have often visited the town and walked past the house where I lived on Church Street. There were also many other places that hold happy memories for me."

Miss Elsie Moore, wrote us a letter, care of The Golden Lion, from Conewood Street in Highbury, London, where our elementary school was located. She wrote: "My elder sister Ras, has just passed me a cutting from the local paper, so I am writing to you because I think I know you. There was a Raymond Pole at school with me and I was one of the evacuees who went through the experience of September 1, 1939. I was at Highbury Vale with my younger sister when I was 12 and she 9. We walked down to Finsbury Park station with our haversack on our backs. I wouldn't let our mother come with us. We boarded the train and were taken to Huntingdon. On the journey an R.A.F. (Royal Air Force) plane flew the length of the train and all of us waved to the airmen, and the crew waved back. We had never experienced anything quite like that before. At Huntingdon we were taken to a hut and given little packs of biscuits, etc. Going to the toilets was also a new adventure for many. These were temporary enclosures made of sacking with small wooden supports over a bucket. From there we were taken to the Corn Exchange (the largest meeting hall in town), and told we were destined for St. Ives. I was billeted in Great Farthing Close and my sister in Little Farthing Close, both of these roads led into Needingworth Road."

"We glared at all the Italians that had been rounded up, not sure if they were prisoners or not, but I do remember they wore large circles on their backs and we were told not to speak to them as they went back and forth to the Catholic Church nearby. I also remember when sweets (candy) were in short supply, eating freshly pulled carrots from a nearby field, not realizing that this was stealing."

"I remember our teachers, Mrs. Hill and Mrs. Keyes and how we attended the local school before we received our own desks from London. Walking the planks along the streets when the river flooded it's banks, made going to school an adventure. One day we walked through the lanes and came to an R.A.F. aerodrome and saw some of the planes up close. I was told later that one night, a German bomber flew over the village and machine-gunned down the searchlight beam. I cannot recall the circumstances, just the incident that happened has stuck in my memory."

"While we were walking back from the aerodrome, a big car pulled up and the lady in the back told the driver to give us a lift. Scrambling up beside the driver, he told us that the lady was the Duchess of Kent. (That Duchess of Kent in 1940 would be the Princess Marina of Greece, the mother of the present Duke of Kent). I guess I will never forget that experience."

Elsie continues, "While many of us enjoyed picking blackberries for 4 pence per pound, we all missed our families in London. Eventually, I returned home in 1942, but my sister stayed on until the end of the war. Our teachers also became our surrogate mothers but as I look back, a terrible void existed when there was little or no nurturing, like when my only brother was killed in the Battle of Britain. Our headmistress had the sad job of telling me and then left me to tell my younger sister."

"I am sorry that I will not be able to come to St. Ives for the reunion on September First." … and so the stories kept coming.

Thelma Merryman (nee Gantry) was most anxious to be at the reunion because she also had later stayed at the home of Mr. Woodhorn, called "St. Mary's" on Needingworth Road fifty years ago, such that we had many common interests to share. Thelma also brought along some of the old school pictures taken in Highbury Vale School of the girls' classes, and we enjoyed trying to remember many of the girls' names. Judy Hess (nee Dawson) remembered my sister Huguette and my brother Gerard when we first came to St. Ives and also later when Huguette went back to London and was enrolled at Tollington Park Central School. Judy recalled how much she had admired Huguette's dancing abilities. Judy is still living in Cambridgeshire.

Joan Clarke related some good experiences with the Londoners as a local girl and can remember well our little gang of boys and girls that use to hang around Green Street. The street is long gone and the houses were all pulled down.

The three Coulson Brothers, who were local St. Ivians, came to the Golden Lion to see if it was possible to recognize anyone after fifty years. While I only remembered brother Pete, the others were able to fill in many details of past experiences. Pete was amazed at the details that I could recall about him as a milk boy, that he had long since forgotten. When I told him how much I had admired the many things he could do as a lad, particularly raising rabbits for profit, and how I use to help him feed and clean the hutches, he couldn't believe it. We had a good laugh, especially how he had showed me what happens when he put the Buck within the Does. The evening was well spent over a couple of pints.

Author's Acknowledgement:

- When I started writing these memoirs I recalled that in 1989 I had come across the publicity initiated by the author, Ben Wicks, who created an unusual occasion to launch his first book, *No Time to Wave Goodbye*, by publishing an open invitation in the press to join him at Marylebone Station on September First 1988. Hundreds of men and women came to verbally share with him their experiences if they had been part of the evacuation day on September First 1939. Needless to say, Ben's book became an instant bestseller. He received so many letters after they had read his book that he decided to compile a second book *The Day They Took the Children* that included ex-evacuees stories and many photographs. This was published for the fiftieth anniversary in 1989.

- I am therefore pleased to acknowledge and endorse these two books published by the Bloomsbury Publishing Limited of London, and to the author, Ben Hicks for his contribution in recording these historic reminiscences.

My first bike and my first pair of long trousers
Age: 11 1/2 – St. Ives Bridge 1940

Chapter Three

Familiar Pathways Retrod

*A*s the reunion date approached, I became aware that I was actually bubbling over with excitement at the prospect of sharing with my wife an experience I had never shared with her before. And now I was to walk down memory lane with her and share a part of my childhood. It is the same feeling of excitement and anxiety that I had when I watch someone open up a present I have given that means so much to me, but I'm not sure if it will be received with quite the same enthusiasm and joy as I am feeling. After months of preparation and days of traveling, we were finally approaching our destination and I became as excited as a schoolboy on his first outing. There were lots of signposts, and I loved every one of them as they counted down the miles to St. Ives.

Beth did her best not to squash my enthusiasm but at times I sensed her feelings which seemed to say, "I hope you won't be disappointed."

I had gone through a similar experience in 1950 when I returned to St. Ives for the first time since I had left. I had come up from London on the train, and my heart skipped a beat when I went up to the newspaper stand of W.H. Smith and Sons but the old man who had been there was gone.

It had been the best paying paper route in town and the only one that provided a bicycle to deliver the papers. At the other shops, the boys had to use their own bikes and arrange their different papers in the right order, complete with all the various periodicals. The manager at Smith's would often help us sort out our papers, and this enabled us to complete our route before breakfast and school.

I smile now as I compared that job to how the paper boys' in America did it. We sorted, in order, a dozen or so different papers and had to ensure that the right combination went to the right letterbox. The boys in America only carry one edition of newspaper, and this is generally thrown from the street to somewhere on the driveway without getting off their bikes. Sometimes it gets thrown from the back seat of their parents' station wagon.

For sure, when delivering papers around an English country town, one had to bike up some very long driveways and deposit the bundle in the correct location; otherwise it would be reported to my boss. That was followed by a very sharp reprimand, and it didn't take too many of those to get you "sacked."

I recalled that in 1950 when I walked down Market Hill, I was conscious of my knees shaking and how hard it was to hold back the tears. It was very embarrassing for me at age twenty-one to be seen crying in the street. I cannot remember what I was thinking or feeling, except that I was full of emotion at the time and very excited to have the opportunity to revisit this special place of my early youth.

It was these same thoughts that crossed my mind as we drove in from Cambridge in late August 1989. Was it just an anniversary that we came to remember or did I have a strong desire to share a portion of my past with Beth? Perhaps, it was to come to terms with the fact that the sequence of events that occurred over these years at such a crucial stage of my 'growing-up' may have influenced the evolving character I was to become.

I expected to drive into town by way of the London Road and cross over the River Ouse via the historic bridge. Instead, we crossed the river downstream and it seemed we would almost bypass the town. The signpost directed us to the city centre but our route took us along the one-way East and West Streets. This way did not appear as impressive to show Beth as I often think that first impressions are so important and our grand entrance was a little anti-climactic. Our one way route took us to the town centre via the Waits. The statue of Oliver Cromwell was still there in the Market Square (thank goodness) so we parked and walked around to get a better feel of what the town's atmosphere had to offer now.

I became very quiet, and Beth did not say a word. I was feeling a little sad that perhaps the town had lost its charm. Beth sensed my disappointment and helped me cope with the reality of time. Perhaps, I had built it up in my mind, beyond reasonable expectations. Of course, nothing ever stands still, and St. Ives was too dynamic and active a place to remain sedentary for so long.

Slowly, the reality of fifty years with inevitable changes began to sink in. We wandered back to the "Anglers Rest," situated along the back-water of the River Ouse at the entrance to the parish church, for Bed and Breakfast. We met the new owners, Philip and Joyce Freeman,. They could see the potential to make this place an attractive gem in this rather unique location.

Seeing the town on a sunny day with so many swans on the river brought joy to our hearts; the flowers on the Waits were a welcome sight. We had become very conscious on this vacation trip around England of the affect that flowers and colourful window boxes can have on one's overall impression and lasting memories. We recalled that towns like Stratford-on-Avon, Bath, and Abergavenny in South Wales had flowers everywhere. Not only shopkeepers but every home seemed to be sporting brightly colored pots of flowers to create a festive atmosphere, and consequently it is most welcoming to the traveler, giving an invitation that says, "Please stay awhile and smell the flowers."

My wife fell in love with the setting of St. Ives Bridge and the view in both directions along the river. She had never seen so many swans at the same time. In fact, someone told us there were now 42 resident swans. I was sure that when I first lived here in St. Ives, there were only two who jealously guarded their appointed territory along this stretch of the river between the locks.

It made sense that traffic was now restricted over the narrow bridge and cars were permitted only in one direction out of the town. The other road bridge over the River Ouse must have been the old railway bridge which now accommodates the bypass road to the "New Town" near the Somersham Road. For me, I preferred the entry to be down Station Road from the new bypass, where the station used to be; thus, one would be greeted formally by Oliver Cromwell when entering the town.

By wandering around, I could see which shops had changed. The little mews and courtyards reminded us of Carmel in California. In that town's main and adjacent streets, every alleyway is enhanced with quaint entrances, flowers, stone pathways and wee shops. People go miles to visit such places. St. Ives has the basic ingredients to do likewise. Rustons' hardware store, along with Kiddles' furniture and Bryants' clothing shop, are now just memories as is Anderson's butcher shop on Bridge St.

Thinking of Rustons', reminded me of another story from the past. One of the boys in our class received an after school job there and quite suddenly he was offering very attractive penknives for sale to all his class mates. While we must have had some idea where they had come from, the price seemed right and the goods were most acceptable, so we all kept our mouths shut. It wasn't too long before an investigation started, and everyone at school was questioned. It was a sad loss to have to give the knives back without a refund for the cash paid, but it was also a hard lesson that had to be learned sometime.

I was moved to see Harry Anderson's shop on the Waits still there, although sadly boarded up for years. The little "Bell" sign outside the late Mrs. Watson's Bar is a precious memory of the past which I am thankful was preserved.

One of the best buildings in St. Ives is still the Norris Museum. It stands proud and strong in a strategic place and presents a good face to the Waits grassy vista. To tarry a while in the museum's garden and watch the swans go by is time well spent. The museum has arranged its contents for all ages to enjoy. Taped music would perhaps alleviate the somber atmosphere prevalent in the museum as if the dead had to be forever mourned. However, I felt thankful and joyful for what the past has given us.

Filling in the arched roadway at the Crown Hotel after the fire must have eliminated the need for a traffic controller who preceded the traffic lights. Likewise, moving the post office from that congested point appeared to have been a sound move.

The new bakery, replacing Stiles, with its additional seating capacity still provides the best place for a quick snack. I am glad that more tea rooms are now evident, especially for market days. The few pubs we visited still appear to retain their unique characteristics and are patronized by "locals," some of whom have probably never tried another bar as yet.

Long ago, I regarded the Golden Lion Hotel as a place where the affluent visitors stayed, and the closest I ever got to its interior was to drop the paper there. On this visit we were fortunate to get a lovely room overlooking the square.

I would offer a special word of praise for the United Reformed Church of St. Ives, formerly called the Free Church. I couldn't believe my eyes as we walked down the Free Church Passage, to see shops coming out of the church walls and a sign out front inviting people in for coffee and cakes. The next day we entered this hallowed place to discover vibrant activity everywhere. Climbing the stairs, we entered the serene entrance to the sanctuary. Wow—what a transformation! We learned how everything had been gutted, the ground lowered, and a new floor added. The organ was moved to the balcony, and many of the organ pipes arranged up the spire. What an engineering feat that must have been! The high arch windows now were at eye level and the nave looked as holy as ever. The niches on either side, containing the elements for communion and offerings, appeared most appropriate. Every piece of furniture was moveable; in fact, before we left the Sunday morning service, all the congregational chairs were rearranged and arm chairs brought in ready for the Senior Citizen Day Care.

The senior pastor, the Rev. Donald McIlhagga, preached a fine sermon for the 3rd of September with the reading from Romans, Chapter 12, on the True Marks of a Christian. He then introduced me to the congregation to express our gratitude to the town and the local people for accepting all the evacuees fifty years ago. There are still some evacuees who made St. Ives their permanent home. It was quite touching when a few members came forward after the service to share their personal memories on that occasion.

The bell tower of the parish church holds many a stirring moment for me. I was fascinated as a boy to watch the bell ringers pull in-time to the caller's patterns. On this visit, I noticed the side pews were missing so I could not sit at my old place where I use to accompany my lady, Mrs Balls. I explained to Beth how the evening service was confined to the main body of the sanctuary and how the lights were shaded to enhance the blackout in those early days of the war.

I didn't mention to her the embarrassment I went through one Sunday evening when, as a choirboy seated in the front row, I wet my pants. Can you imagine my feelings as I watched the trickle creeping across the floor of the sanctuary. My face has never been redder than it was on that day.

I was pleased to see from my touring of England, that many tomb-stones have now been relocated around the periphery of the grave-yards surrounding the churches, giving up the space for lawns or a memorial garden. I am hoping that it won't be another fifty years before the elders will allow the tombstones around the Parish Church of All Saints to be repositioned. This would allow for a more pictur-esque setting, particularly since the walkway is constantly used as a public thoroughfare. The newly painted iron gates with their gold tips were a sign of hope for a more picturesque setting.

How many people living in St. Ives today would know the location of Barnes Walk? It is the pathway from Church Street that runs parallel to the backwater towards the thicket. There never was a name sign but it was an address for those three charming little cottages at the end of the walk that have disappeared, together with the boat access to the back-water. The ford crossing to the island was still there and so was the rickety bridge to the original swimming pool which has now been converted to a haven for the Sea Scouts. What luxury today, to have a boat harbor and a club house, just for Scouts.

Barnes Walk appeared much narrower now perhaps because the trees along the waters edge have grown so large. The only street light above the foliage did not illuminate the path very much but probably pleased the lovers who use to cuddle and kiss along the wall. When I ran home to one of those cottages and there was no moon, I was afraid to imagine that arriving at the wrong moment would be a good reason for getting hit or even tossed into the river by an angry suitor.

The three cottages have since been demolished but they did belong to the Cropley's big house at the back. The approach to the river where Mr. Hunt kept his boats is now fenced off and it now looks a little drab and wild. Again, something unique and picturesque was lost to the bulldozer. It was such a special place for me that I could only now describe to Beth in words. The feelings of loss and nostalgia stayed with me for a very long time.

I always felt that the pathway through the thicket was also very inviting for both pedestrians and cyclists. Beth and I wandered down the path for old-time's sake. I did sense that in those days, it was very traditional and pleasant for many locals to take an evening stroll, with or without their dogs and go down the thicket.

While the erection of wire fences to prevent trespassing into the osiers may be an eyesore, it was probably good that the Scouts were now responsible to protect this haven of adventure. This location use to be a battle ground between the young kids and the high school kids, or between the Londoners and the locals as regards rights of access.

The pathway to the bird sanctuary has become worn and broken with the passing years. Perhaps the councils involved will do what they can to preserve this precious foot and cycle path to Houghton. The ceiling in the bird sanctuary seemed much thinner now, and I wondered what birds ever found sanctuary in this once-beloved haven that was leased for ten shillings per year.

It was my understanding that the island on the River Ouse, was to be a perpetual sanctuary and with the backwater running parallel to the Waits, it should always be navigable for non-powered boats. It appeared that in 1989, to be in danger of being blocked by overgrown brush from the island and underwater weeds from the bank. This stretch of water was certainly a charming location to linger by the grassy area of the Waits, and St. Ives cannot afford to neglect this natural treasure for future generations.

Chapter Four

How I Spent My Spare Time

I must have been quite happy not to have been taken back to London since my parents thought that I should not interrupt my schooling, and besides I had become quite acclimated to my new surroundings. From the Sims house, I moved on to the Rev. Springham's home which gave me a greater perception of life and a larger circle of acquaintances through the Springham's ministry. At first, I had a pal in their son Robin, until our relationship deteriorated and became hostile; nonetheless, I also had more freedom to choose my friends.

I got my first job after school with Barton's, the Chemist shop on Bridge Street. Yes, it was Mr. Barton Sr. who appeared to have a perpetual dewdrop on the end of his nose. The old man was very kind, but I received my daily instructions from Mr. Armitage. I had to sweep out the store and on Saturdays, polish the brass plate on the outside of the shop front. When the business and building sold fifty years later, that plate was moved to the Norris Museum.

Every afternoon I would load up the basket onto their big carrier bike and proceed to deliver around town and sometimes to the surrounding villages. Invariably, my basket was full of wines and spirits, as well as flagons of soda syphons, destined for the gentry of our neighborhood. In addition, taking much less room and weight, were the prescriptions and toiletries. I really enjoyed my employment, but alas someone found out that it was illegal to employ a boy under 12, so I was "sacked." The pay, I believe, was in the order of three shillings a week, which helped pay the installments on my bicycle and still gave me money for the pictures at least twice a week.

Feeling the pride, satisfaction and independence of earned income, I yearned for more work. Somehow, the extra jobs around the house that yielded payment were never very exciting, and I must have felt resentful, particularly if Robin got more pocket money for less work. That was about the time when I wandered onto the Anderson Poultry farm on St. Audrey Lane and worked my way into a paying position.

I was also attracted to the pony and trap and our local milkman Syd Clements, who worked for G.P. Bradford of Hemingford Grey. Syd would drive around the houses filling milk jugs from smaller cans, which in-turn, were filled from the milk churns on the trap. While milk was delivered every day, dairy products such as butter and fresh eggs were delivered two or three times a week. To help Syd was a 15-year-old lad by the name of Peter, a person with whom I became very friendly. He, looked so grown up with his big gum boots, peak cap, and a pail on each handlebar of his bike. He would also go around the houses giving out milk but he moved much quicker than Mr. Clements who also had to drive the pony and trap.

It was pretty evident that they needed some help, so it wasn't long before I became a part of that team. What joy and exhilaration I felt, when Mr. Clements finally allowed me to move the trap a few yards down the road; it must have surprised the pony! How I wished all my classmates could see me in action, but, of course, I was not allowed to drive the trap home through the town. I got to know a lot of people this way, and besides having fun, I was able to earn a little money as well.

Summer of 1940 came, which meant no regular school, although, to keep us all occupied and out of our homes, we had recreational school.

This comprised singing, plus arts and crafts and much storytelling. It wasn't so bad for three hours a day. In the afternoon I was off on my bike to join my gang of friends.

The swimming pool on the island was opened then, and much time was spent there whenever it was warm enough. One day, one of our classmates swam "umpteen" laps across the pool to reach a mile, a feat that was envied by all. I still remember that he did the breaststroke, and he developed a black mark on his upper lip from constantly blowing air out in natural river water. Two or three years later, the authorities closed the pool for being technically unclean, although I didn't see anything wrong with the water. After all, there was a wire screen at either end to keep out the fish, ducks and other debris, but tiddlers did get through. So perhaps the breaststroke was the best way to swim after all!

Getting around the local farms, I got to know who was picking what and when. My favorite fruit was the plums, especially greengages, but eating too many would soon make me ill. They were easy to pick and the baskets were quick to fill. Currants-red, white, and black were not so plentiful for commercial buyers but they still had to be harvested. Apples and pears were not so prolific, besides they did not ripen until September after we had gone back to school. Soft fruit pickers were always in demand for gathering gooseberries, strawberries and raspberries.

In the autumn, we "picked up" potatoes. It was a backbreaking job and one that was closely supervised. We were not left on our own, as with fruit picking, since we had to keep up with the horse-drawn plough.

Haymaking was the most fun. After the thrasher or cutter mowed the hay and raked it into rows to dry, we had to gather armfuls to tie into bundles and stack into piles. When we gathered wheat, corn, or oats, it was a similar procedure (at least it appeared that way to me), but they had to be stacked carefully in pyramids with the ears up, whereas hay could be piled together in stacks. The "meadow" ran along the east and south of the River Ouse from the St. Ives bridge for about 4 miles and was a half mile wide. It was a glorious sight to behold when it had been freshly mowed, and the hay was drying. It smelled so good that on a warm evening many people would go for walks through the meadow.

I can recall my first pangs of passion, as I lay in the hay one day, staring up at the blue sky, fantasizing on sexual pleasures. I wasn't yet thirteen, but I was experiencing the feelings of being deeply aroused. I was very much in love with a girl called Mary at the time, and all the kissing and cuddling was beginning to evoke even stronger feelings. I can also recall that I was going through a tough period of passionately kissing my pillow at night. However, we did enjoy an evening stroll down Meadow Lane which was also known as "Lovers Lane."

It appeared that at times, our gang members were talking a lot about sex. I guess we were all experiencing similar feelings even though we never really knew all the details. Our gang was a fairly tightly knit group. There were George Johnson, Stan Mullett, and myself, and our respective girl friends: Edna, Pam and Mary.* Although sometimes we were out of favor with our sweethearts, most of the time we were all together. We had many other friends who came and went; one special person was Dinky Wheeler who was also stuck on Pam but the main group stayed very close for quite awhile. All the boys were Londoners so we had much in common, but I'm not so sure the local boys were pleased with this intrusion.

A lot of spare time was spent in the "Osiers" plantation located on Ingle Hott island which was a simple step across the field alongside the thicket path just south of Barnes Walk. While playing cowboys and indians would appear rather immature, creating bows and arrows from the osier vines would become very realistic and even dangerous

---

* I often wonder where these old friends are today and how interesting it would be to read about their life stories.

at times. We would also build very intricate huts by threading the vines into an igloo. Unfortunately many hours of hard work would be smashed by rival gangs, which I found very distressing. One day, while exploring and looking for new tracks in the dense jungle of osiers, I found an intact hut that had been occupied by some older boys. Inside were paper and wood, a fire lighter and briquettes, books and magazines, cigarettes and matches, and a "French letter." Wow, what a find! Of course I was scared, in case any of the owners would suddenly appear while I was inside. I left promptly to tell of my find. Unfortunately, it didn't last too long, for a week or two later, I discovered it had been smashed and the contents of the hut taken.

We would sit for hours, just two or three of us (sometimes six or seven), talking together about sex, or our problems at home or life in general. Then we would get bored with that and decide to play hide and seek games, or even "postman's-knock" and other such romantic games, if the girls were with us. The London parks had no place like this.

Another great pastime was "bird nesting" in the spring. I would wander for hours along the hedgerows, peering through the branches or searching along the river banks for a new nest. I would never take all the eggs, but invariably steal two, one to add to my collection and one to trade. If there were not at least two eggs, I would take note of its location and return later.

It was in the same fields that I would later gather blackberries to sell for sixpence a pound to a local housewife who would then resell to stores or take them to the weekly market. In the course of a season, I must have picked over forty pounds—another supplement to my weekly income.

The many pubs in St. Ives seemed very attractive places to us, not only because of their individual characteristics but because of the camaraderie of their "regulars." In fact, these regulars were hardly

ever seen in any other pub, except perhaps on market day when people moved around to where the action appeared to be. Most of the
locals knew where certain people could be found and if not, either the
barman or other regulars would know their whereabouts.

I remember as an assignment for school, I wrote down the names
and location of all the pubs in town; maybe there were fifteen to
twenty, which I thought was pretty remarkable for such a small place.
However, I have been told that around the turn of the century, there
were over 70 licensed outlets, which only goes to prove the success of
the local market and fairs in those days.

If one really wanted to rediscover the past and to sift through the
biographies, recollections and "I remember when ... " stories related at
the local country pubs, one would learn how history was made and
deals were finalized.

Not being of drinking age, the pubs were just a curiosity for me in
those days, and a good place to buy a packet of "Smith's Potato
Crisps," complete with a wee pinch of salt, wrapped in a twisted piece
of blue paper, and maybe a glass of fizzy lemonade to wash them
down.

Chapter Five

Auntie's Cottage and the Boats

*H*ow was one supposed to address new foster parents? I cannot remember what I called my new foster parents while living with the Sims or the Springham's. When I was billeted with a wonderful widow, she made it clear that I was to call her "Auntie." I was quite relieved as I was not very comfortable with her name—Mrs. Balls.

Alice Balls had been widowed for about twenty years and entered "service" (short for domestic service) as a cook until her mid sixties, and by 1940 she must have been way over seventy. Alice had helped her late husband run the Crown Inn in the neighboring village of Earith. They had lost their only daughter at age eighteen. Mrs. Balls took in another boy by the name of Jimmy after I left and she became quite attached to him, particularly since he did not appear to have had much of a home life. Jimmy must have stayed for three or four years, and I was glad that Auntie had someone else to love.

Life was very pleasant in Auntie's cottage at #3 Barnes Walk. There was a comfortable sitting room, although most of the day was spent in the small kitchen, which had a brick floor. We had no electricity but did have a gas stove and a gas mantle.

The "outhouse" (always scrubbed spotlessly clean) was at the bottom of the garden and was shared with the old lady next door. In our little garden, we were able to grow quite a few vegetables for our daily needs and still had room for beds of flowers.

A tiny flight of stairs curled to an upper landing where I had my bed, and Auntie occupied the only bedroom with her wire-haired terrier Trixie. The sitting room included a chest of drawers, and I was allocated two of these drawers, one for clothes and the other for all my precious belongings.

I was given the scary job of filling and cleaning the paraffin oil lamp with its tall glass chimney. I remember the portable wireless set and its wet cell battery which had to be taken up to the town for recharging. When the days were long and dreary, Auntie would knit "socks for soldiers" and she taught me how to do tapestry. Another favourite pastime on sunny evenings was to stand at the gate and watch the people go by on their way down the thicket, many of whom were locals, and some would pause to chat awhile.

I came back looking for Auntie in 1954, and after many inquiries, located her in a State Hospital in Huntingdon. She was walking the grounds, but her heart was weak from a severe heart attack. I was nervous that seeing me would set off another tremor, but she laughed with joy when I greeted her. I was anxious to show off my secondhand Wolesley car but the doctor said the risk was too great to take her for a ride. Alice Balls passed away a few months later. It was people like Auntie that made the evacuation program work.

Miss Laird, our next door neighbor at #2 Barnes Walk, was gone by the time I returned in 1950. Apparently she went to sleep one night and never woke up. What a way to meet your Maker at 95! She had a strong constitution and a stubborn will, a reflection of her Irish heritage. She would insist on going down to the waters edge to bail a bucket of water, and one was never quite sure what she did with the water.

Sydney Hunt, the fisherman lived in the first cottage on Barnes Walk with his grown-up daughter Angela. On the other side of the pathway in front of the three attached cottages was a dock area, and this was the "tie-up" for Mr. Hunt's boats. The slip could accommodate 6-10 rowboats and punts and a couple that could handle an outboard motor.

I wasn't paid by Mr. Hunt, but I did enjoy his company and would help to clean the boats, bail out water, and do anything for a free ride on the river with him or alone. He was hired out by the hour or by the day for fishing trips and he taught me how to fish, but I lacked the everlasting patience that he possessed. I admired him for bringing in many a roach or perch and sometimes even a tench for a meal. In winter the prize was a 2-3 foot pike that was exciting to see stuffed and prepared for the oven. While Mr. Hunt had his moody days, he tolerated me and we were close friends.

The Hunt's finally moved out and took over the Limes Boarding House located at the corner of the Waits and Ramsey Road and renamed the hotel "The Anglers Rest." I was told that this building was the original grammar school for girls, while the boys had the Priory. The boats and the guest house slowly deteriorated after Mr. Hunt died. His daughter Angela died in 1979.

Angela's husband finally sold the property in 1989 and the new owners were anxious to renovate the site to its old splendour and recapture the river trade that was so much a part of St. Ives.

In those days, some competition in the way of punts and row boats came from Dynes Boats uptown. The big business for the river, I believe, came from the many house boats that paid to come through the locks. These holiday makers would tarry a while and visit the town before going through the next set of locks by the Houghton Mill.

Through Mr. Hunt, I met a couple with one child on such a house-boat, and the family "adopted me" for quite a few days. I loved being adopted much to the consternation of "my lady," (an endearing term we used when describing the lady with whom you were billeted) who never knew when I would be home for meals. When I did come home, it was not long until I was away again. Adventure on a house boat was not to be missed. Of course, I never realized my indiscretion until years later, when she was describing my successor as being quiet, reliable and was always home for meals. It was on such an escapade, that I got one of the best pictures I ever took on my two-shilling camera.*

This photo which portrayed this gorgeous houseboat on the river was my pride and joy. I gladly showed off my "work of art" to my new found friends and to anyone else that could be impressed.

The river scene was always charming and could be seen from many vantage points, such as the locks, the quay, the bridge, the meadow, the Waits and the Houghton Mill. It was very tranquil to observe a slow moving river, particularly in the early morning or in the late evening before the sun sets. A spectacular sight, at a certain time of the year was a flight of swans over the meadow, following the course of the river … and how they would honk to each other during flight.

The river was not always calm and serene, and once in a while during the spring tides, the water rose and kept rising way over the wall on the Waits and up to the street. It was certainly a different experience to walk to school balancing on raised planks. Barnes Walk, being very

---

* It was purchased from F.W. Woolworth's in Huntingdon at a time when nothing in the store was priced over 6d-(-the reason it was also known as "Three pence and tanner store"). The plastic camera was priced out as 6d for the front, 6d for the back, 6d for the built-in lens, and 6d for the #127 film. One would view the object through an open rectangular frame representing the 2 1/4 x 2 1/4 film size.

close to the backwater, could only be reached by boat or with thigh length waders. The cottages were just high enough to escape being flooded out.

Chapter Six

My Church Life

I would like to share some aspects of my church life during my stay in St. Ives, for it was certainly active and varied. One tended to go to the denomination of one's foster parents; it was easier that way and less complicated. Going to church was something to be endured by most boys, but I found enough variety to make it fun; besides I received a lot of affirmation there. Perhaps it really was a very good ground base for my faith which I finally claimed in my confirmation by the Bishop of Stepney, before my sixteenth birthday.

While I was billeted with the Methodist pastor, the Rev. Springham, I naturally went along with the denomination of his family. Mr. Springham ministered to three churches: Houghton, Hemingford Grey and, I believe, Fenstanton. Traditionally there were morning and evening services on a Sunday and invariably, I had to pump the organ if the verger was ill or away, as well as other duties as needed, such as ushering. Mr. Springham was kept busy cycling from one town to the other in some sort of rotation. Most of the time, the family cycled along to at least one service, especially on Sunday mornings. Houghton was the best because we could then bike through the thicket.

Returning fifty years later, I was a little surprised to see the chapel in Houghton had gone but relieved to see a new church in its place as part of the reformed church of St. Ives.

When I lived with Mrs. Balls, I attended the St. Ives Parish Church with her, particularly since it was so close to her cottage. She used to say she wasn't going to do all that "bobbing up and down" (genuflecting) but neither was she going to walk to the Free Church up town. The music was interesting and different so I joined the boy's choir and stayed for over a year.

Our church in Highbury, London, was classified as a "low" Church of England, whereas the St. Ives Parish Church was "very high" and was often referred to as Anglo-Catholic. It was rather foreign to me at first but, like everything else, "we went along." The order of service was the same as our London church, but they sang more and the Holy Communion service seemed quite a pantomime to me, especially the shaking of the incense and the bell ringing at different places during the service. As a choir boy, this meant more things to learn to sing. Sometimes the discipline of attending three times on Sunday plus a practice during the week was time consuming, and my friends said that such a routine would drive them "batty" (crazy). Of course, we got paid, a pittance maybe, but then we didn't know any different and dutifully made our minimum attendance quota. Father Hum, the curate, was very approachable but it seemed the head pastor, Father Newell, hardly gave us any notice.

Who has ever stood and watched bell ringers pull in time to the pacer in a village or small town church? The routines which the pacer called, causing the bell ringers to pull in sequence, were always very fascinating to me, and the bells rang for 10-15 minutes twice a day on Sundays. I trust this tradition will never die in England as it has done in California.

This church was very old (at least fifteenth century), and it did have an impressive altar with a long aisle which was good for processions. Like so many churches of that age, the atmosphere appeared dull and it took a lot of stirring music to make it come alive. The graveyard surrounding the church contained three pathways which were also used as thoroughfares for pedestrians. The entrance to the church had a deep stone-covered porch with bench seats on either side. I would always run past this porch on my way home on dark nights, and nervously flash my torch. Invariably the light caught a loving couple cuddling in the porch. One moonlit night I got really scared when I heard something behind a gravestone—sure enough, another couple....

The Free Church was really my favourite and, while I was never obliged to go, it was there that I felt the most comfortable. The minister, at that time, was Neville Britton, who appeared to have a good relationship with our school teachers. (That was good because we were using their facilities for our day school.) We sang as a group but did not have to dress up in cassocks and surplices, complete with a stiff collar and a clip-on bow tie, which was the tradition at All Saints Parish Church. The Free Church building was quite modern, by comparative standards, being only 120 years old.

On special occasions I would visit other non-conformist denominations, such as the Wesleyan, Methodist, and the Baptist Chapels. Wandering around nowadays, I noticed the following inscription outside the Baptist Chapel: "This is a Strict and Particular Baptist Church" which stirred my curiosity with an unresolved question "What is this all about?"

Chapter Seven

Market Days

St. Ives has always been a market town with medieval fairs going back a thousand years. It was hard to go to school on Mondays because of the activity everywhere around town. Before school, after school, and on holidays, I would be drawn, with or without my friends, to the cattle market to listen to the peculiar jargon of the auctioneers as they went from pen to pen obtaining their bids for the cows, bullocks, sheep and pigs. Occasionally, a horse or two and even some bulls and a few goats were put up for auction. Then I would move on to the poultry and produce market (which is now a car park) to see the chickens, bantams, roosters, rabbits, and any other small livestock submitted for sale to the highest bidder.

The produce came in a variety of types and quantities, perhaps a few pounds of fruit and vegetables from individual growers to many crates from the produce farmers. I believe anybody could take anything to the market and with a numbered tag, have each item auctioned to a variety of bidders. The "bric-a-brac" was a collection of everything else.

A momentous day in my life came when Mr. Springham brought home an old bike for me for which he had bid ten shillings. It was nothing fancy, but it looked sturdy enough. Riding his own bike, he steered the other home with one hand. I was ecstatic to have a bike of my own! I had always borrowed my mother's when I lived at home in London and it seemed a pain to be always asking permission. I paid Mr. Springham two shillings and sixpence and made up a payment book for the balance at sixpence or a shilling a week. This came from my income of wages earned from household chores or many other jobs that I was able to do. I remember well, rubbing the bike down with emery paper and painting it blue with white mud-guards. Eventually, it was finished, complete with bell and a basket.

All the country people had baskets on their bicycles, for there was always much to fetch and carry—something city folk could never understand. Now I was mobile, and that wonderful vehicle took me miles around town and to the surrounding villages, and enabled me to earn considerable income over the next two years.

In the main street, called Market Hill, market day would attract many stalls of food, clothing and hardware and even the conventional shops would put out goods for sale. It was an interesting experience that was new for me and is still going on.

This weekly gathering of the cattle and produce markets and to witness the auctioneers hammer, is apparently no more. Maybe this is because people have cars and trucks to take them where the animals, poultry and produce are located, rather than vice versa. Perhaps something of intangible value has also been lost in the process.

Relating about the animals, I can still recall the many hours I used to stand outside the slaughter house in an alley-way off East St. By peering through the slits of the windows I could watch the whole operation and the sequence of events associated with the slaughter of pigs and sheep. It was both a fascination and perhaps morbid curiosity. Sometimes I would feel sorry for the victims being slaughtered and at other times, I admired the men and the competency with which they carried out this necessary task. What a noise the pigs made with their incessant squealing. I'm sure they all knew what was going to happen to them. After the shot was fired into each pig's head, a long slit was made in their throat and the pigs were then dragged across the floor and allowed to shake and quiver while all their blood flowed freely around the floor. They were then thrown into big wooden tubs of hot water, and after a soaking, each was strung up for skin scraping and disembowelling.

The sheep did not go through the shake and quiver routine, being placed on hooks for skinning after they were shot and before they were opened up. For country folk, I guess this was "everyday stuff," but for us city boys this was a new world of experience and gave us a better appreciation of how our food was prepared for the table.

Mr. Harry Anderson, the butcher, had his slaughterhouse in the back of his house on the Waits but had long ceased to kill his own meat. The rings were still around the wall near the floor, which he told me were used to pull the steer by a rope threaded through the ring in his nose and through the ring on the wall. This routine brought the animal into total submission before it was killed.

There was a larger slaughterhouse in town, and I remember once giving the slaughter-man there some "cheek." He chased and grabbed me and then carried me upside down around the slaughterhouse, rubbing my nose along the various entrails and offal that were hanging around before he finally lowered me down into the inverted belly of a bullock as it was just about to be opened. The last act of punishment was a head dip into the hot tub where the pigs were thrown prior to scraping. When I stopped screaming, I ran all the way home to wash off all that slime and smell.

Auntie thought it was very amusing but I was humiliated, and notwithstanding that terrifying experience, I now had to strip off all my clothes and wash down in a basin since there was no bath or shower in the cottage. That incident did much to curb my "cheeky" disposition, and I definitely kept my distance whenever I revisited that slaughter house. What a story I had to tell my pals after that incident.

Chapter Eight

School and After School

*T*he area around St. Ives attracted a lot of "gentry" in those days These select families inherited property, went to the "private" schools and colleges, and maintained the prestigious businesses of the town. I used to know most of them by name, even if they didn't know me, because I had delivered to their homes, either the morning paper, their meat, or their "spirits." These homes were often set within large grounds or estates and the families maintained a staff of servants. Occasionally, the gentry would host a garden party or a garden fete. A garden party was more formal with maids running around with drinks or trolleys with tea and cakes. The garden fete, on the other hand, was an open affair that encouraged stalls and games in the name of local charities.

On these occasions our Headmaster, Mr. Lockeyear, was invited to bring his chosen choral groups to entertain the guests. "Locky," as we called him, enjoyed that style of English music and spent hours training us to sing *Where E'er You Walk* and *Greensleeves* which were part of our extensive repertoire. He used to spice the program with enjoyable numbers like *"Knick Knack-Paddywack, Give Your Dog a Bone* and *McNamara's Band.*

This selection of music was such a contrast to the style from our former Headmaster "Mickey" Marchant, who performed himself in many musical comedies. Being a part of a repertory company was Mickey's hobby. He would delight us with excerpts from the musical *Hiawatha*, in which he performed regularly at the Royal Albert Hall before the war, plus many other interludes from his varied repertoire. The annual children's Christmas concerts at our school also before the war, were thus very professional affairs, being produced, directed and written by Mr. Marchant. One year he produced a minstrel show, and I can still recall the excitement of dressing up with huge white bow ties, burnt cork faces and painted exaggerated white lips. Later, he produced a sequel with a Mississippi style like chorus when I was the lead singer. My Mother spent a lot of time making my costume and she was very proud of the whole performance.

Mr. F. T. "Mogy" Stanley and Mr. "Jumbo" Jarvis were two of our teachers who were also evacuated together with their families. "Mogy" was so named because he walked with a cane and he had a steel plate in his leg, an injury that he had sustained in the first Great War. How his nick-name came about is hard to tell, but it had been passed on from class to class for many years. It still surprised me to learn from his fourteen-year-old son who joined our evacuated school that Mogy always knew about his nickname; so he was called Mogy Jr. We became very cautious about sharing too much with him. lest he told his dad later at home. One day, when he got the cane from his dad along with two other boys for normal classroom mischief, he then became "everybody's friend."

Mr. Jarvis was a very kind person and had the youngest age group of the boys' school. His class, like most classes, was made up of two age grades, spanning the ages from 10-15. (The legislation had just changed the school-leaving age from 14 to 15 for all elementary schools.) "Jumbo" liked country dancing and he taught us the Maypole dance which we performed at many garden parties

Mr. Pierce, a teacher from the Blackstock Road School (the school we merged with on evacuation day) loved to read stories out loud in class.

We did a lot of that at the beginning because we had little in the way of school equipment and a regular curriculum. A book I remember with warm sentiments was *Wind in the Willows*, and Mr. Pierce enjoyed verbalizing each character with lifelike eloquence.

When we first arrived in St. Ives, we used to assemble at the local school, alternating morning and afternoon sessions with the St. Ivians. This did not work out so well; perhaps the local staff as well as the students resented their facilities, desks and books being shared by strangers who had been thrust into their midst. Thinking back, I am sure that very little thought was made to acclimatize both teachers and students from both schools until after incidents just happened.

When we had school in the mornings, we did gardening in the afternoons, or played organized games, or sometimes were taken for a school hiking trip. The gardening consisted of tilling rows of vegetables, digging, hoeing, weeding and harvesting. This was a new experience for many London kids, and we learned the lesson of cleaning our gardening tools until they were spotless.

One day, I pierced a garden fork through my shoe and into my big toe. Although I told the "Master" (*how we referred to our teachers*) how much it hurt, he probably did not realize how serious this was. When I got home "my lady" pulled off my blood-soaked sock, saw the puncture in my toe, and promptly took me to see the local doctors. Dr. Grove Snr. and Dr. Grove Jnr. had been assigned to care for the medical needs of the evacuees. Although Dr. Grove Snr., who may have come out of retirement to make this "his war effort," was well known for his sharp tongue to his patients, he seemed to have a genuine concern for us kids. I was impressed when he let me know that he was going to "tell that teacher off" who let this accident go unreported. He warned me of the potential dangers of "lockjaw," and this warranted a tetanus shot in the "you-know-where." What's more, this injury qualified me for three days in the "sick-bay," a miniature hospital set up in the Methodist Church Hall on the Waits. What fun to be visited by many school friends, as I was confined to bed but feeling great! Even my teacher sympathized, no doubt after the scolding he had received from Dr. Grove.

The produce we grew on the school allotment was sold very cheaply to our host families to supplement the weekly "allowance" given to them by the government for the support of each child.

Most local working families in the country had "allotments" which were plots of ground in a community area where they grew their annual supply of vegetables, since many families did not have big enough gardens within their homes to sustain their year-round needs. At every home in which I lived, I was expected to spend some time working on the allotment, which was not always fun especially when the weather was bad. I tried to get a plot for the widow lady, saying that I would do all the work for her, yet not realizing this would have been a burden instead of an asset for her after I left. The garden at the cottage did well to augment our daily needs. Each of the allotments had a little shed, generally covered with corrugated iron, which contained the garden tools, wheelbarrow, etc. and also provided a place to wait out the rain, which came quite often.

It was in such a shed some years later that my very good "local" friend hanged himself. When I had returned in 1950 for a weekend in St. Ives before emigrating to New Zealand, I went to find "Mort" Chambers who lived in Oxford Close. No one seemed to know a "Mort," since this was his nickname and I had forgotten his real name was Maurice. I found his grandmother, and before she even told me, I seemed to sense something had happened to him. You can imagine the shock when she confirmed my fears—such a tragic death for this fine eighteen-year-old boy for whom life had become somehow unbearable. I got to know Mort because he was the same age as Robin Springham, with whom I had lived on Cemetery Road. Robin and I seemed to be constantly fighting. Being bigger and a year older than I was seemed to give Robin the right to bully me. I must have found some refuge with Mort and his gentle spirit, because we often went off together on our bicycles, away from Robin, for some peaceful adventure.

Life with the Springham family was not all fighting, although there was a lot of tension within the family. Being part of a minister's family did not absolve us from problems and Robin appeared highly strung at that age, while his younger sister Olive was a sweet little girl. One of my duties was the chopping of kindling for the copper fire in the kitchen. The copper was a built-in concrete sink with a copper lining and a fire grate underneath to heat the water to wash the clothes. In London, my mother had a gas "copper" which was a very tall, cylindrical galvanized tub placed on the gas stove to boil the clothes.

At the Springham's, every week, I also had to wash the red stoned tiled floor in the kitchen. I used to think that Robin had easier jobs to do, or perhaps I perceived them to be easier at the time.

My reward was a small allowance and oat-cakes, a delightful concoction made with porridge oats, margarine and sugar, and then baked in the oven. Robin and I slept in the same room overlooking the cemetery and I would gaze out of the window on to the newly dug graves and wonder what all this meant; another new experience to ponder. I became quite fascinated by the activity and the comings and goings that occurred in a cemetery. Quite often, we would take walks around the tombstones to read the inscriptions and make judgments on how well the graves were being maintained.

Opposite the Springham's Manse, was Mr. Day's estate. I'm not sure whatever happened to that lovely house and garden. I was equally surprised to see that the house rented to the Springham's had been pulled down, and a police station now stands on its former location. Cemetery Road was renamed Broad Leas.

I was also surprised to observe that a whole new scheme of homes had been built on the sites of the Westwood "Anderson" Farm and on the All Saints Vicarage land in the area of Church Street and Westwood Road. One of the houses still standing on that corner used to belong to a Mrs. Watts. My host lady, Mrs. Balls, would often go to Mrs. Watts to assist the kitchen staff and help prepare dinner for special occasions. Through their relationship, I got the job, three nights a week for an hour or so, tidying the garden, doing many odd jobs that the gardeners did not do, which included cleaning windows.

A few doors down the road on Church Street lived Miss Katie Stiles with her aged mother, and Miss Hunt, her cousin, lived next door. They were both wonderful women, and Miss Hunt was, later I believe, commended by the Queen for taking in so many evacuees. There were as many as ten children of all ages being cared for, many of whom had no other home, and some were refugees from Europe.

Miss Stiles was the Billeting Officer after Freddie Favell and she bore the brunt of the sustaining work for much of the war. To constantly find new homes and to respond to all the problems conveyed from the host families, the evacuees' parents, the schools and the kids themselves, must have been a thankless job that never ended. The praise and recognition they both received was truly earned. Incidentally, Freddie Favell, at 86, was present for the 50th anniversary. When I interviewed him, he could remember well, not only all the incidents that occurred on September 1, 1939, but many of the episodes beforehand. He related that the task of finding homes and selling a new government program was most difficult. No one really knew the complete plan or all the ramifications involved. Being also the deputy town clerk, Freddie developed a remarkable memory for knowing the town's history and a working knowledge of all its occupants.

Mr. George Anderson, Sr. was the local farmer of the town. Two of his sons, George and Harry, became butchers, and another son Jerry, stayed the farmer's boy and eventually took over the family business. When I lived up the Ramsey Road with the George Sims family, I spent many hours on their large poultry farm on the corner of Ramsey Road and St. Audrey Lane, where Jerry had to look after hundreds of chickens. There was an old railway carriage parked in the middle of the field and Jerry and I would do a lot of talking in one of those compartments when it was raining. Another compartment contained all the feed, another was used for tools, and still another for plucking the chickens. Jerry taught me how to pluck without tearing the skins, but I never did master how to wring a chicken's neck. He did it so fast; it was as if he enjoyed the power this gave him when he needed to finish an execution that I had started in vain. Gathering eggs was a far better job than taking the chicken swill around the chicken coops.

Another good Anderson was young Peter, who was two or three years older than me and he was then living with his grandpa "Old Harry" in a small house opposite the council houses where I lived with the Sims. Old Harry was very kind and jolly and looked the real old fashioned farmer in his jodhpurs. He drove a pony and trap, and whenever he saw me, he would always give me a ride.

Mrs. George Anderson had also taken in some evacuees and was always generous with her time and attitude towards us all. Mrs. Anderson was a strong woman, who had to be reckoned with, and ran her household with earned respect from all her family and friends

Once Mrs. Anderson rescued my brother, Gerard, when she found him wandering around the cow sheds. He had deviated from his long walk home from school at the Constitution Hall (which was being used as a school room) to the top of the Ramsey Road. We had all done that walk so many times that we soon learned the art of hitch-hiking to help make the three-quarters mile, two or four times a day, go quicker. Even for the older kids, it was still a tiring and boring journey and any deviation along the way was tempting. The open farm gate was all the invitation that Gerard needed.

Nostalgia ran high for me, when fifty years later, Harry Anderson's butcher shop on the Waits was still there, complete with his name on the tiles as part of his frontage. (I hope photographs of his shop go into the archives of St. Ives.) Harry had no front window since the front was open when the shop was open and shuttered when closed. Harry would converse with everyone passing by and cut meat to order. He had a full-time eighteen-year-old delivery boy named Jack Saunders who rode the carrier bike which enabled him to deliver many meat orders for delivery every day.

I was the part-time daily errand boy, who made the local deliveries during the week, but I had to do this by balancing a wicker tray on my handlebars. The meat and poultry was not covered but exposed on a thin white grease-proof paper on the tray. Each order had a tag pinned to it bearing the customer's name, price and description of the order. I remember well when ice was on the roads and my bike would slip beneath me, I went flying. Away would go the chops and the chickens etc. sliding down the road. I tried to clean the meat with my hanky and restore some order before delivering same. Occasionally an extra piece of meat would be left on my tray and not knowing to whom it belonged, found its way into my pocket to be presented to "my lady" as a contribution for our next meal.

Although we had ration books, the butcher allocated out the available quota of meat given to him amongst his registered customers. This was well augmented by un-rationed rabbits, hares, chickens, sausages and other strains of offal by those that could afford it.

On Fridays and Saturdays Jack had to help Harry in the shop, so I got the "big bike" but also got the big routes. This was a good fifteen mile circuit to Hemingford Grey and Hemingford Abbotts, and all around the surrounding villages. The weekend was the time for the roast joints and big birds, but deliveries of fresh meat had to be made two or three times a week since only the rich people had refrigerators. It took ages to go to many of those big houses, and around the driveways to the kitchen door. The heavy load was hard work for a twelve year old particularly if the wind and rain were beating in his face. On cold and wet days, the cooks would often give me a hot mug of tea and biscuits or something nice to keep me going.

Some nights Jack and I would have to go into the back room to make sausages, which was a cold job even on a warm day. This is where I learned where sausage skins came from.

I was also paid extra by Harry's wife to look after her chickens, feed the dog, or do some other small jobs. Their grown up daughters were "smashers" (a slang word meaning very attractive) from my vantage point, and they constantly teased me. They appeared to lead a fun-loving and exciting life as girls in their early twenties.

Reminiscing about the gentry of St. Ives, I am reminded of the special people that I came quite close to, particularly Mr. and Mrs. Savery, who lived on the Broadway.

Mrs. Savery was the daughter of the Copley family, who were a very influential entity in the town for many generations. Mrs. Balls, who was noted for her good family-style cooking, was invited along with her ward (that was me) to cook for the Savery's Christmas dinner and the Boxing Day buffet.

Mrs. Savery, in her wisdom to keep me occupied and less bored, took a liking to me and showed me how to lay and wait on tables, so that I was well-schooled before Christmas Day. I would respond to the call of a tinkling bell to pick up dishes or serve clean ones, and she always appeared considerate that we had enough time to eat our own courses in the kitchen. By the end of the Christmas Holiday, I was well indoctrinated and everyone was pleased with my performance in "butlering."

From that time on, I used to watch for Mr. Savery taking his dogs for a walk down the thicket and "catch him up" to grasp the opportunity of conversing with him on all sorts of worldly affairs. I think he enjoyed these encounters with a young evacuee boy as much as I did with a country-style gentleman. When I returned to locate the Savery's house, it appeared that parts had been remodeled and an interesting type mews had been added. I never did find the kitchen and courtyard that were there when I was there.

Chapter Nine

Dad's Ride

*B*efore the war, personal cars were considered a luxury for most working class families, and since Londoners always had adequate public transportation, the automobile never became a necessity. It certainly was the age of the bicycle, a form of transportation that became universal whether for convenience to get to school or work or pleasure. My dad rode his bike back and forth to work, twice a day, from North London to the Strand for twenty-five years. It wasn't so much the distance of five miles, but rather the hazards of the traffic that created the challenge. One had to contend with cobblestones, fast electric trolley buses, trams and tramlines, lorries and many horse-drawn vehicles, besides other cyclists and pedestrians.

I can remember the times on a Saturday afternoon when I would meet my father at work by borrowing my mother's bike, making the same hazardous journey to the Strand so that we could ride back together. Perhaps we would stop by the open air market in Chapel Street, Islington, to pick up some meat and vegetables for Sunday dinner and make another stop by the newsagents and tobacconists shop to pay for the papers and where Dad would buy his Woodbine cigarettes. Traveling by bike was a precarious and dangerous escapade, but growing up with London traffic, I became streetwise at a very early age.

When my dad would cycle a hundred miles to be with us while we camped on the East Coast of England, I used to think that he was "Super Dad." I was particularly proud of his lapel pin claiming membership in the "National Cyclists Association." With the demands of his work, only one day off per week, and the growing anxieties of the possibility of the war escalating, it was very difficult for Dad to visit me in St. Ives.

One early summer's day in 1940, Dad wrote to say that he would cycle to St. Ives by getting up really early on the Sunday morning to make the 60 mile journey. Can you imagine, going on a journey with no sign-posts to guide you? The authorities had taken them down so as not to give any help to a potential invader or even to an enemy parachutist.

I was so happy to see him and to show him my town and surrounding countryside. I must have gotten carried away because I was able to persuade him to go for a "bike ride" to pick blue-bells. That was at least another 25 mile round trip. Poor Dad! He never complained, and I regret so much my thoughtlessness. I was unaware of the sacrifice and effort he had made to get there at the end of a hard week's work. Dad, I am sure, would have been pleased to sit in a boat and be rowed up and down the river, but I had to take him all over the country so as to keep him all to myself. I know that he really did enjoy our one-on-one visit, because he mentioned it years later.

I am sure my dad must have pulled over, on his lonely journey home, and had a "wee nap" in the bushes. I loved my Dad very much. He was very unassuming, shy and friendly. He was very proud of his family and forever grateful to my mother for her strength and dedication to the family.

I became very anxious when I learned that he had been "called up" for the army and then his special visit with me in St. Ives became even more, a treasured memory. Although he had been assigned to head-up the field kitchen of a RHQ (Regimental Head Quarters) because of his classification as a Chef, he later became injured by shrapnel from our own guns that were interceding the German Doodle-Bugs crossing the coast on their way to London.

Dad and Mother finally came to California to be near us and spent the last ten years of their lives together. It was a real joy to see Dad be so happy in his new environment.

Chapter Ten

Yes! There Was a War Going On

*I*t was more than a year after evacuation day when the bombing started on September 7, 1940. Over 300 enemy bombers with 300 tons of high explosives and several thousand incendiary (fire) bombs headed for London. Being only sixty miles away we, in St. Ives, saw the red sky on the horizon. With BBC newscasts reporting every hour, we began to realize the vulnerability of our homes. The news reports just stated which area of London was hit the worst which was little consolation to those of us who were only wanting to know that our street was spared and still intact. This was really a very scary time for me and for most of the other London kids. Perhaps for the first time, we really began to feel the empathy from the local people as they attempted to understand our heart-wrenching concerns. We felt trapped, with no personal news by telephone or mail and did not know what to do.

Letters were not very frequent, and later we understood why. With the traumas that people were experiencing every night to find shelter from the bombing and then dragging themselves back to work, or managing the home, letter writing was not on the agenda. Since most people did not have access to telephones, a phone call was not to be expected and the majority of homes here did not have phones either. So we just had to wait for news.

Week after week, the air-raid warnings were sounded every night in London and life must have been very hard for the Londoners. Later we learned that other towns and cities such as Coventry, Clydebank, Newcastle, Birmingham and all the industrial centres were also targeted. Because we were never made aware of the vulnerability of these areas in Britain, it never phased us in the same way as our familiarity with our home town of London. On December 29, 1940, it appeared from the news on the radio, that the city of London was about to be razed, but from the newsreels being shown at our local cinema, seeing the dome of St. Paul's standing high and proud as a Christian fortress, warmed our hearts with pride.

Another institution that stood firm amongst the chaos was the "Old Lady of Threadneedle Street." (*This building represented the principle legal authority in Britain.*) The Law Courts and many of our ancient and traditional monuments in and around the City defied all odds. We learned that 50,000 people were made homeless and several thousand were injured. The indomitable spirit of our leader, Mr. Winston Churchill, inspired ten million people in greater London to hold together and "never, never give up." There were times that I must have felt that I was missing all the action, but when the gory details became known to me, the sanctity of the quiet countryside was a blessing.

At the beginning of the war and bending to publicity from the authorities, my mother created a gas-proof room in our London home, such was the level of fear prevalent at that time. Not only was the fireplace sealed, but so was the keyhole in the door. Losing the use of this room was a problem because it also served as a partial bedroom. The intensity of the blackness, plus the lack of fresh air when the windows were closed every time the air-raid warning was sounded, created a lot of discomfort. So with the passage of time, the feeling of complacency and common sense took over, the gas-proof room was reopened for general use.

As the war progressed, Mother converted the cellar into an air-raid shelter as the fear of being bombed out became a greater threat.

We lived in a typical London terrace three-story house, occupying two levels, with a spinster and her dog in the top story. The cellar measured about four feet wide by twenty feet long, at the end of which was a coal chute from the street level. Four cots were strung up to accommodate the spinster lady, an elderly lady who was living alone next door, and my sister and brother. Old rugs and blankets were hung on the walls to insulate against the dampness. The coal was shoveled to one side to allow access or egress through the man-hole cover in case of an emergency.

Mother, a senior uncle and sometimes my dad (whenever he could make the journey from work in the West End) would go into the cellar and sit on the steps when the bombing got bad. Everybody felt safe and as secure as could be, since there were few alternatives. Some people dug holes in their gardens and installed the Anderson Shelter, which was often cold and damp, since it was hard to keep the rain and water seepage out. People with money, built reinforced rooms with the help of a Morrison Shelter, a cast iron framed table, to allow two or three people to crawl into and, thus, be somewhat protected from falling debris. Others made the daily pilgrimage to the "tube" stations and made themselves comfortable on wire cots that were provided along the platforms after the trains stopped running.

By the time the Battle of Britain had started in the fall of 1940, 20-30% of the evacuees had returned to the cities illegally, that is, without the sanction of the school authorities. Since there were no schools open and with everybody preoccupied with the air-raids, many of the London kids became wild without any supervision, particularly if their mothers were doing some sort of war work and their fathers had been called to the armed forces.

Our neighborhood in North London escaped the devastation that the East End suffered, and the children, although largely unsupervised, did not really become a threat to law and order. Nevertheless, the London County Council finally took action and brought back some of the teachers from the evacuated schools to open the London schools, in order to get the children off the streets.

Our house in Highbury Quadrant was situated near the center of three nearby parks, creating a lot of defense activity in our neighborhood. In the largest park, the Army positioned a huge anti-aircraft gun, which produced showers of shrapnel whenever it was fired, some of which came through our windows and pierced the black-out paper. The other two parks had barrage balloons, which were used to keep the enemy planes at a higher altitude.

Life in London, during this period, which continued for over a year, must have been extremely stressful, but the Londoners stuck it out with determination to get through the crisis. They even managed to find much to laugh about, thanks to the encouragement of many comedians and the variety shows that were constantly being broadcast.

There was little else anyone could do because most people had no place to go that could provide any additional shelter, and they still had to work to earn enough to survive week by week. The crash program to build reinforced brick and concrete shelters in the streets came about after most of the bombing had subsided. It must also have been a relief for the majority of Londoners, knowing that their kids were away from the battle zone and were being taken care of, even though the separation must have been painful at times. While the circumstances were not ideal, most people accepted that the alternatives could often be worse.

When the enemy became occupied dealing with battles on many European fronts, things became a little more normal in Britain and, in fact, quite pleasant at times. In 1941, our country was then "teaming with "Yanks" (*Americans*) preparing for D-Day." They brought with them, powdered eggs, spam, plenty of gum for the kids, silk stockings for the girls, and a pocket full of money, all of which made them heroes to a large cross-section of our population.

Factory girls would put tan make-up on their legs and even get their younger brothers or sisters to draw a straight line with an indelible pencil to simulate a seam, such was the fashion in those days. By the end of the war, nylons made the scene, so the scheme of bartering became more prolific.

With two large airbases nearby, St. Ives was also inundated by the "Yanks," so now the locals could shift their attention from the evacuees to their higher paying guests.

I think St. Ives has earned its place in the history books, maybe not as material for a school primer, but for the number of times the status quo has been changed to disturb the quiet town and its ever-changing town folk.

Chapter Eleven

Now A Teenager

*T*he time had come for me to move on, and in 1941, I was transferred to a London High School that had been evacuated to Luton in Bedfordshire, an industrial town some thirty miles north of London.

It was very painful for me to leave St. Ives. I promised to write and said I would return. Saying goodbye to my girl friend was very emotional and, although only thirteen, I felt my heart would break. I had become acclimated to this small country town and the thought of starting all over again, in new surroundings with no friends, filled me with anxiety.

By passing an exam, I earned a place at the Day Technical School for Boys, a division of the North Western Polytechnic. The school was home-based in Kentish Town in the north of London and was now sharing space at the Luton Modern School, a grammar school for boys. Our grade levels spanned over three years from 13-16 years of age. We intermingled in the use of all the local school facilities but retained our autonomy as regards our own teachers and curriculum. The masters of both schools wore their academic gowns, and the local boys wore their school uniforms.

Because we were evacuees, our school did not insist on uniforms although we were encouraged to wear grey flannel trousers (short or long), a black blazer with a school crest on the pocket, plus a black cap with a crested school pin.

The headmaster also acted as the billeting officer, which must have been quite a chore for him to cater to the housing needs of some 200 boys. He had found a very nice home for me with a young childless couple in nearby Stopsley, but I was broken-up when they informed the headmaster that I had to leave, just as I was beginning to make friends with my new classmates who lived nearby. I never knew the reason for their decision but got the impression from my friends talking to their hosts, which perhaps they resented the sudden intrusion on their privacy and had been carried away by the persuasive powers of our headmaster.

My next home was miles from the school on the other side of town, with the Adams family. Mr. Adams had a delivery route for a local brewery, and Mrs. Adams worked at a straw hat factory, which was the town's basic product before the war.

Their fifteen-year-old son Geoff shared his bedroom with me and attended the local technical school. The third bedroom was shared by two factory girls who had been conscripted to Luton from Yorkshire to do war work.

Later the Grandma came and stayed in the "front room," so you can guess we had a houseful in this modest three-bedroom terrace house. I seemed to fit in well with everyone although Geoff appeared to enjoy the status of being older and, at times, invoked the privilege of being the bully. Perhaps this was because his older brother was away in the armed forces, and his role was now reversed.

After about a year, tensions in the house were building up and I felt the need to move on, so this time I set about finding my own billet. Through my paper route, I got to know a mature brother and sister who had set up house when the sister's husband went overseas. The brother was the chauffeur to a local "Lady," and their house was on the grounds of the estate. The sister was employed as a housekeeper to a larger family and I was fairly content for another year or so.

The highlight of my stay with this family was being invited to spend a summer holiday in their home village of Wickhambrook in Sussex. Living in a real farmhouse, feeding the animals, and joining the villagers in the evenings to go gleaning in the fields, was my idea of a good holiday in the country.

My last home away from home was with an elderly church-going couple who were quite strict in comparison to my previous hosts, but who gave me much love and attention.

Highlights of my high school experiences were centered around girls, school dances, and the Army Cadet Force. Somehow I must have appeared much older than my years, a situation I enjoyed, but it backfired when the girls I dated were graduating and I still had a year of school to go. We looked forward to the school dances with budding musicians forming swing bands which were very popular at that time. I can vividly recall that for fun we would climb to the fourth floor square balcony of this local Technical College and look down the well at all the dancing below. Being fairly dark on the balcony, it was a good place for smooching.

The Cadet Corps took a major part of my after-school activities (as did my morning paper route, my only source of income). We had general assembly for two hours after school twice a week. Being issued regulation army uniforms may have helped with our clothing needs but the fabric was rather coarse and the neck bands seemed to be ten times bigger than our size 14 necks. Our school masters were the officers and the senior boys, through merit and favor, became the NCOs. I guess I was the proverbial clown who was often caught "cutting-up" until one day, on the weekly posting of the "orders for the week" appeared the statement, "Private Pole promoted to acting Lance Corporal."

No one could believe it, least of all myself, that someone would recognize any worth in me. Later, I was to discover the psychology of such a move, and it apparently worked! With this recognition I changed my attitude and was promoted to full corporal within six months. I enjoyed the feeling of standing in front of my squad of six cadets and issuing commands during marching drills, or being in front of the classroom explaining the maneuver of a frontal attack in a make-believe battle. I felt so good about this role which created the idea that perhaps I could be a teacher when I grew up.

Since our school was at the edge of town surrounded by countryside and hedgerows, it was great place for field exercises, complete with survey maps, to play at war games. This was better than marching up and down the parade ground with heavy boots and carrying fake wooden rifles. During the summer break, we went to a regular army camp nestled in the Cotswolds, which is located in the west coast county of Gloucestershire in England, for a two-week concentrated army course with real army discipline.

Living in barracks, doing KP (*Kitchen Patrol*) and completing a full day of intense activity, was tough but fun—another growing-up process.

One of the goals of the camp was to pass the classification of the "red star" for achievement, which by its merit, permitted one to wear the cloth star above the NCO stripes. It was a proud day when we all returned to school to be recognized as those who had passed the test.

I chuckle to myself now when I think how brazen I was to appear before the ticket office at the local railway station, dressed in my khaki uniform but wearing a white shirt and tie, (I could not afford to buy a military-type shirt and really only officers wore ties) and then ask for a "Forces Return to London." Most times they issued me the special rate ticket to enable me to go home for the weekend, now that the blitz had ended.

Another very special merit was the "brass crossed-swords," earned by passing the test as a "physical training instructor." This was a grueling course at the Hendon Police Academy in North London and involved everything from an obstacle course (designed for grown men), two hours guard duty, (I drew the 2-4 AM. shift), a five-mile walk in one hour, and competitive swimming in the nude (another first for me). During this two-week intensive course, which we all thoroughly enjoyed in retrospect, we had two 4-hour passes, and I remember well the big treat of meeting my folks for dinner at the Lyons Corner House in the Strand. Of course, I felt good, being in uniform when this appeared to be the normal dress at that time, particularly in the west-end of London.

Sporting our "brass crossed-swords" on our sleeve when we got back onto the parade ground carried a great feeling of pride and accomplishment.

As a closing reward for all graduating cadets, we were invited to be the guests of the real army for ten days. Since I had now become a Sergeant Instructor, I was assigned to the sergeant's quarters of the former Eighth Army that had returned from the desert war in North Africa. Soldiers were resting up prior to new preparations for the D-DAY assault on June 6, 1944.

The camp was located on Lady Astor's estate somewhere in Berkshire, and since maneuvers were off, these Army veterans filled the time recounting many incidents from their experiences in the desert, which kept me in awe.

I was taught to ride a motorbike and wasted no time going for practice runs around the country roads, dressed up in helmet and goggles as a regular "Don-R" (Dispatch Rider). I ate in the sergeant's mess and was invited to the NCOs parties. I think they forgot that I was not yet sixteen (I was kind of mature for my age!).

This was also my first encounter with a prophylactic which I discovered was standard issue from the quarter-masters store. I really felt grown up when I was able to take a few packets back to school for trade, for it was something one could not buy as a young teenager. I guess it was also a status symbol, in those days, to have one hidden in your pocket.

I completed my full-time day schooling and returned to my home in London to commence my five-year indentured engineering apprenticeship. I was unprepared for the adjustment of returning to the control and influence of my mother who was not prepared for my grown-up status. My uncooperative attitude didn't help when I was anxious to claim my presence as "head of the household" now that my father was in the army. My uncle, who had been part of our household since 1939, and had really given so much support to my mother during the hard times, created a situation that I resented and which eventually caused a lot of problems at home.

Not being in London during the blitz, it was an adjustment to be suddenly confronted with the horrors of being bombed. It was nerve racking to experience the "Doodle Bug" (V1 rockets) raids. One of these "Bugs" appeared to be chasing me up the road one day while I was cycling to work and that was terrifying. When I heard the motor cut off, I jumped off my bike and dived into the bushes in someone's front garden. Thank goodness, it landed in the middle of an empty cinema just three hundred yards behind me, thereby containing the blast.

These "Doodle-Bugs" were pilot-less rockets that flew at fairly low altitudes with their rocket engines spurting flames out of their rear. The noise and their appearance were most intimidating to the civilians as these "Bugs" would come and go for days. If the engine stopped overhead, you were safe since the rocket then glided in a parabolic path to the ground and exploded. Attempts were made to give us warning whenever they had crossed the coast, but in the end, we were never quite sure if the air-raid sirens were still on "alert" since it was hardly ever an "all clear" situation. My Dad was serving in an "ack-ack" unit (a battery of anti-aircraft guns) near the south-east coast, trying to shoot them down. Later, when the V2s started dropping, there was no evasive action, and no air-raid warnings, only the experience of being shaken by large explosions at any time of the day or night. V2s flew through the stratosphere and fell very fast.

One such V2 rocket nearly got me. I was in London between the Highbury Barn and Highhbury Corner when it crashed into a block of flats right across from the Grammar School. Yes, I was badly shaken by the nearness of the explosion and my first reaction was to run towards the site to see what happened. Dust was rising as a cloud but there was little other noise. The sudden stillness was frightening. Where were all the people? Glass and small debris was everywhere. Staring at the ruins, I wondered what happens to all the furniture and clothing and linen when a house collapses. Then I bent down and picked up a small piece of wood and a tiny piece of rag. It was later confirmed to me "that's really all there is left of someone's home after being hit by such a blast of that magnitude." It was not long before the police, fire and ambulances were on the scene and I was told to go back beyond the created barriers.

I was at home now after five years of surviving the evacuation experience. Since that experience occurred during a maturing stage of my life, it really did have an influence on my character and development, both consciously and sub-consciously. Although this was not realized till years later, I have always felt that it was a good experience for me and one that left a lasting impression.

8th June, 1946

T O-DAY, AS WE CELEBRATE VICTORY,
I send this personal message to you and
all other boys and girls at school. For
you have shared in the hardships and
dangers of a total war and you have
shared no less in the triumph of the
Allied Nations.

I know you will always feel proud to
belong to a country which was capable
of such supreme effort; proud, too, of
parents and elder brothers and sisters
who by their courage, endurance and
enterprise brought victory. May these
qualities be yours as you grow up and
join in the common effort to establish
among the nations of the world unity
and peace.

George R.I.

This certificate was given by His Majesty, King George VI to
every child who attended school and was evacuated.

Epilogue

T hirty five years after the war, Clive Sinclair (now Sir Clive Sinclair) took over the old paper mill in St. Ives and brought consumer electronics as a new industry to the town. He also brought new inventions to the nation and the world in the form of miniature calculators, televisions, pocket telephones, and numerous other items including an electric car for children. Even in today's fast moving pace in the electronic world, technological breakthroughs are occurring so often that their origins may be overlooked in the passage of time.

St. Ivian's Association

There exists an association of record whereby all people who were born in St. Ives are eligible to become members. Included in the rules, is the statement that "persons who were evacuated to St. Ives during 1939-1940 were also eligible for membership." I was pleased therefore to qualify for a membership card and proud to be a member.

I trust the escapades and memories of a very young boy as an evacuee, sixty eight years ago, along with the nostalgic recollection brought about by revisiting this historic and significant town, will be well received by the local St. Ivians.

I acknowledge The Friends of the Norris Museum who have done a wonderful job of preserving the history of St. Ives by documentation, photographs and identifying the many people who have contributed so much to make this country town so unique and interesting.

It must be some basic Puritan heritage that still prevails in St. Ives that has kept it modest and serene. My appreciation to the current historians and the curator of the Norris Museum to ensure that St. Ives, which is now in Cambridgeshire, maintains its visibility on the map.

Appendix

Oliver Cromwell Made a Difference

*U*pon reflection, I sense that many people in Britain are really unaware of the significance of Oliver Cromwell and even perhaps by the population around St. Ives. His home is preserved near the entrance of Ely Cathedral so the tour guides would mention this fact on passing the cathedral. However, it is in the town of St. Ives, situated in the original Shire of Huntingdon, that you will find a statue of Oliver Cromwell, and thereby hangs a tale that is worth recording again.

The inscription on this fine edifice in the town's square states, "A Townsman of St. Ives 1631-1636." Most inscriptions on statues carry the dates of birth to death, but the dates on Cromwell's statue only covers the period of his residency in St. Ives. While Cromwell was not born or died here, St. Ives is the only place that displays a statue to perpetuate his memory. History books have treated him, rather ambivalently in terms of his importance, but he did contribute very much to the basic premise of democracy as we know it today, both in Great Britain and around the world. Even then, politics and the power of influence, determined that many decisions may never get resolved.

Little is known of the ceremonies in 1901 when the statue was dedicated, but we do know that Cromwell's birthplace was in Huntingdon which was a royalist right wing town at that time. The townspeople of St. Ives were sympathetic to Cromwell's Puritan heritage and claimed the recognition of Cromwell for themselves.

Oliver Cromwell was a brave and deeply religious man, who fought for many years against what he believed to be the tyranny and injustice being exercised by the King of England, Charles I. The common man was not guaranteed freedom and justice in those days and when the people were being exploited by the few in power; it took a courageous man to rise up and fight for these basic rights that we take for granted today.

Cromwell was born of a noble family in Huntingdon, the county seat, in 1599. His uncle was Sir Oliver Cromwell and his grandfather, Sir Henry Cromwell.

Young Oliver did some schooling at Cambridge University but had to return to tend to the farm after his father died. While studying law in London, he married well to a rich merchant's daughter. In 1628, Cromwell was elected as a Member of Parliament for Huntingdon and there he became familiar with and involved in the affairs of state which were anything but peaceful at that time.

Charles I became a tyrant. He collected taxes without parliamentary consent and imprisoned many for not supporting him financially. After much protest from Parliament, the King dissolved the House of Commons and all the members returned home to plan a revolt. Eleven years of unrest followed, until another Parliament was convened; but meantime, bands of men were joining together to stand and fight for the freedom and the right to be governed by representatives of the people.

St. Ives came into the picture when the King became aware of the fertile farming ground in that area which could yield good crops if there was better drainage. So he ordered and paid to have drainage implemented. He then took the harvest yields and some of the land and gave them to his favored friends. Cromwell, a country farmer, publicly responded vehemently and gathered favor with the people of St. Ives to protest against the King's actions.

The greed of the King continued, and to get more he decided to reconvene Parliament. Now the resistance was stronger and a civil war between the King and his government was inevitable. The people of England were divided. Those who were ready to fight for the King lived mainly in the North and West of England, while those who were determined that the country should be governed by their representatives in Parliament came from the East and South.

Cromwell gathered an army of common people and soldiers and joined the Earl of Essex to challenge the King and his army of rich men and nobles at Edgehill in Worcestershire. Cromwell's foot soldiers were no match for the King's cavalry and withdrew to raise more horse soldiers. By now, both armies had grown to twenty thousand men. Skirmishes and small raids were going on all over the country, presenting constant turmoil and unrest until a deciding battle was fought near York in July 1644. Cromwell's well trained soldiers, who were also known as the "Ironsides," drove the King's army of horsemen, known as the cavaliers, from the field, and won that battle.

Thousands lost their lives with the King's men taking the greater loss of fourteen thousand. The final battle between these two groups took place at Naseby in Northamptonshire in 1645.

Many attempts were made to make peace with the King, but each time, the King was found to be untrustworthy and was forever trying to make treaties and deals with anyone who would believe him.

Finally, Cromwell was able to bring the King to trial, and the court of Westminster found him guilty of treason and had him executed.

For eleven years Cromwell tried to keep the peace in Parliament as well as to appease "all the King's men" throughout the country. Although many of his followers wanted him to be king, he knew that as the "Lord Protector" he would have more power than a king. He also knew that for stability and freedom, the country should be governed by a Parliament chosen by the people. Cromwell still hoped to restore the monarchy as a constitutional power under his terms. Cromwell's way of doing things angered many a parliamentarian such that he still had just as many enemies, even though he was the victorious strongman. He managed to survive many attempts to assassinate him.

Oliver Cromwell took on the garb of a Puritan and dressed in simple clothes compared to the King's followers who dressed in colorful silks and velvets with fancy plumage in their hats. The men of that period had traditionally long hair, while the Puritans cut their hair shorter and became known as the "Roundheads."

The Puritans were generally quiet and sober in their speech and habits and strictly observers of the Sabbath. The Puritans were against the Anglo-Catholic form of worship service, which had succeeded the Roman Catholic era during Henry VIII's reign, and wanted to "purify" and make "simple" the church services by taking out any mention or rulings created by the King. This was the beginning of the break-away non-conformists tradition.

Cromwell was a deeply religious man and believed everything he did was inspired by God. He was respected and trusted as an honest man and by his belief and actions, set the stage for all freedom loving democracies to this day, and so changed the course of English history

It was as a Puritan, that his statue in St. Ives portrays him, with his back to the Church of England's Parish Church of All Saints. Carrying a Bible in one hand, one wonders what he is pointing to with the other hand! The statue, erected in 1901, marked the 300th anniversary of Cromwell's birth.

The invasion of St. Ives by the evacuees from London, in 1939, was followed three years later by the Americans from the surrounding airfields. While no different from what was happening all over the country, this probably changed the character and significance of the town as it had done some three hundred years ago when Cromwell decided to live and work in this non-conformist town of Saint Ives.

Authors note: Information relative to Oliver Cromwell was gleaned from Dr. L. du Guarde Peach's book on Oliver Cromwell and published by Ladybird Books Ltd., and from the "Official Guide to St. Ives" written by R. I. Burn-Murdoch, Curator of the Norris Library and Museum and published by Ed. J. Burrow of London.

Oliver Cromwell
A Townsman of St. Ives
1631-1636

Sketch created by David Ogilvie from a photograph, 2006.

About The Author

Returning to London after being evacuated for five years, I spent my youth serving a five year indentured apprenticeship with the British Thompson Houston Company in Willesden, London, working in a factory and attending part-time school at the Willesden Technical College. I also had time to enjoy the privileges of being a Youth Club Leader. At age twenty-one "I took off" by emigrating to New Zealand, which in 1950 took six weeks and three days by sea, with a few interesting stops on the way.

In Wellington, I was assigned to the State Hydro-Electric Department as a Junior Engineer and completed my engineering studies in Mechanical & Electrical Engineering at the local technical college. While in New Zealand, I was able to explore some of the mountains and back country of both islands as a member of the Tararua Tramping Club.

I returned home to London in 1954, working my passage as a ninth engineer aboard a freezer ship. When I discovered that my old school and work friends were now wildly scattered, I then accepted an assignment with the Sudan Mercantile Company in Khartoum, the capital of Anglo-Egyptian Sudan. This was a great experience (prior to the British flag coming down following the Suez crisis) before returning again to London in 1956.

There I met my future wife Beth Ogilvie, and we got married in 1957, and decided to go to Canada. Beth was hired by Cunard and I started with Westinghouse in Montreal but after a year of enjoying all the four seasons, Westinghouse had a large lay-off and we took this opportunity to visit America. With very little funds it was prudent that we apply for a resident alien status so that we could have a "green-card" to obtain temporary employment.

We visited my sister in Houston, Texas, and since neither of us were truly happy in such a different environment, that it was not difficult to accept an invitation from a friend of Beth's, to come to Palo Alto in California. We thought California was heavenly and we made our home in this area for another 48 years. We have two children, four grand-children and were most fortunate that both of our parents joined us for their retirement years in California.

978-0-595-40876-4
0-595-40876-1

Printed in the United States
69375LVS00004B/250-285

9 780595 408764